Real Fairies
True Accounts of Meetings With Nature Spirits

David Tame

Capall Bann Publishing

www.capallbann.co.uk

Real Fairies
True Accounts of Meetings With Nature Spirits

©1999 David Tame

ISBN 186163 0719

Cover design by Paul Mason
Internal illustrations by Damian Bland

Published by:

Capall Bann Publishing
Freshfields
Chieveley
Berks
RG20 8TF

Acknowledgements

My grateful thanks go to all those who granted permission to quote from their publications. Permissions were granted by Vija Bremanis and Quest Books for *The Real World of Fairies* by Dora Van Gelder and *Fairies at Work and at Play* by Geoffrey Hodson; by Dorothy Maclean for her chapter in *The Findhorn Garden* by The Findhorn Community; by Tanis Helliwell and Blue Dolphin Publishing for Tanis's *Summer With The Leprechauns*; by Alice Meyer and Droemer Knaur Verlag for Marko Pogacnik's *Nature Spirits and Elemental Beings*; and by Michael McNeil and Norman Millman at Summit University Press for the unpublished Mark Prophet material (thanks to both Michael and Norman for patiently fielding my requests).

Special thanks are due to my wife, Faith, who lent support and practical help to this book in many ways. Damian Bland not only provided the wonderful illustrations, but has always been a sounding board of crystal clarity on this and other subjects. In a sunny rural English setting in May 1997 I discussed such a project as this with Neroli and Peter Duffy, and chapter 24 simply would not have happened without Peter's searching through the archives to find and send me transcripts of Mark Prophet's lectures. I am also so grateful to Peter Dawkins for the delightful interview - and for learning what our ego-balloons are really for. Finally, my acknowledgement of deep gratitude to Oromasis and Diana, Aries and Thor, Neptune and Luara, Virgo and Pelleur, and all the beings of nature who serve under them, without whom we could not write or read this or any other book, for there would be no platform of evolution in which to do so.

Other books by David Tame:

The Secret Power of Music
Beethoven and the Spiritual Path

Contents

1

The Kingdom of the Fairies

Twenty-three 'fairy stories' are collected together in this book. But these are not mere folklore, or fictitious bedtime reading for young children. No, the accounts that follow are told by sane and sober men and women who actually believe they have seen and communed with real fairies.

Almost all the accounts are told in the first person, in the witness's own words. The reader can make up his or her own mind as to the veracity of these accounts, of course. But after reading these accounts, the reader's opinion may well be that even to call these experiences 'alleged' would be to do a disservice to the experiencees and to the reports themselves. In each instance, that the individual is honestly recounting in plain language what they firmly believe to be the truth - that they were totally in control of all their faculties and were not imagining things at the time - seems obvious. But what are we to make of these reports?

One thing is clear: if people are increasingly willing to believe that such accounts may be true, and if many people today do believe in the existence of fairies, this is not a new phenomenon. Outside of the prevailing western culture and its largely reductionist-materialistic scientific world-view, there may be no other society on earth, past or present, that has not accepted the reality of fairies or nature spirits.

Records of humanity's belief in the existence of nature spirits are as ancient as history itself, and are universal. There are the many widespread tales, fables and beliefs in fairies from Britain and Europe, and accounts of meetings with the "little folk" or leprechauns of Ireland. The ancient Greeks, Romans, Egyptians, Chinese, Indians, the North American Indian tribes, and other peoples also believed in goblins, sprites, satyrs and other beings of nature. Each river or fountain had its nymph, the air had its sylphs of the skies, and the earth was peopled with fauns, dryads, and brownies. Nature spirits are still held in the highest esteem in some parts of the world, where propitiatory offerings are made to them. In Iceland, where Christianity did not become the official national religion until the eleventh century, the majority of the population still believe in the 'little folk': homes are not built, and roads skirt around rather than go through, any area that clairvoyants say to be inhabited by them.

Today we see a growing interest in fairies as we enter the new millennium. Movies such as *Fairy Tale* and *Photographing Fairies* have brought the subject back to mainstream attention. And this present volume is by no means the first recent book on the subject to be published. However, fairy experiences take many forms. The people who have such experiences also interpret them in different ways. Moreover, should some form of clairvoyance be involved, it seems as if the nature of this clairvoyance may differ from one person to another. Thus, some clairvoyants see fairies at a different level or in a different way to others. One of my purposes in releasing this book is therefore to demonstrate the variety of fairy experiences.

The accounts that follow are each one person's way of attempting to describe encounters that at times may be almost indescribable. If one person's words cannot convey what such experiences are like, perhaps we can gain a better

2

idea by listening to a number of accounts, and from a variety of very different people. By putting them together I hope to create a broader and better picture of the whole - a better apprehension for the reader of the realm of the fairies.

Experiences from times both distant and very recent are set forth in the following chapters. Paracelsus (chapter 15) and Cellini (chapter 7) both lived several centuries ago, while the observations of Marko Pogacnik (chapter 22) date from the 1990s. Some of those who tell their tales are not normally clairvoyant, and only had one experience of this nature in their lives. Indeed, in some cases, such as William Munro's (18) sighting of a nature spirit at Seaside Head, it is not at all clear that clairvoyance of any kind was involved or needed. Other witnesses, on the other hand, such as Geoffrey Hodson (17) and Dora Van Gelder (16), were not only naturally and deeply clairvoyant, but put their abilities to use in very carefully describing and categorising every form of fairy life they were able to observe. They apparently were able to see and commune with fairies on an almost daily basis. Again, the various witnesses also differ in that some of them, such as Scottish sheep-farmer Alexander Gunn (19) or the unnamed farmer's wife in Somerset (4), were otherwise quite ordinary people lacking any worldly fame. On the other hand, poet, artist and mystic William Blake (8) was one of the greatest and most unusual talents of the nineteenth century.

But what is a fairy?

I will leave it to the witnesses themselves to answer most aspects of that question, but to begin with it is worthwhile explaining that there are two quite distinct uses of the term 'fairy'. First there is the typical fairy as depicted in children's books. This is that archetypal sprightly form, usually depicted as feminine, with gossamer wings and a slim physique, perhaps holding a wand, and possibly flitting from plant to plant. This is what most people today are thinking of when they speak of 'fairies'.

However, such fairies are only one kind or 'species' of an entire lifewave of intelligent beings that includes gnomes, elves, undines, leprechauns, goblins, brownies, tree spirits, sylphs, and all such spirits of nature. At around the beginning of the twentieth century, clairvoyants who investigated such nature spirits named them all under the generic name of 'fairies'. Hence, in this use of the term, a sylph of the air or the spirit of a tree is a 'fairy', as are gnomes, brownies, and all the others. I have called this book *Real Fairies* with this second sense of the term in mind.

There seem to be thousands, perhaps millions, of different kinds of fairy or nature spirit. Therefore a taxonomy of the nature kingdom would have presented complex problems had not clairvoyants since the time of Paracelsus realised that all fairies belong to one of four distinct categories. Just as the alchemists of old spoke of the four 'elements' of Fire, Air, Water and Earth, so every fairy belongs to one of these elements also. It not only lives within that element, but the very function of the fairy is to work with that element to which it belongs.

In speaking of Fire, Air, Water and Earth, we are not referring to those substances or energies we normally use the words for, but rather we are speaking of their inner, subtle essence. Thus, for example, the alchemical element of water is not water such as we drink, or wash ourselves in (though it will interpenetrate that tangible, visible water). Rather, it is a spiritual essence - the unseen essence, as it were, from which the physical water derives. Some nature spirits are fairies of the water element, and are all classified as *undines*, even though within this kingdom of the undines there are nevertheless hundreds of extremely diverse types of being. Similarly, earth-element fairies are all classified as *gnomes*,

4

though not all look like the traditional gnome-like figure. Fairies of the air are called *sylphs*, and fairies of the fire element are *salamanders*. Since gnomes, undines, sylphs and salamanders each dwell within their own appointed element, they are all more commonly referred to today as *elementals* rather than as fairies. To avoid confusion with the more typical and definite fairy-like being, I shall from this point use the term elementals, rather than fairies, in referring to the nature spirits of all the four elements. (The typical, classic fairy being, by the way, is usually a part of the gnome kingdom, strange as that may sound, for they work with the earth element.)

The scientifically-minded may be curious to know just how 'solid' the body of an elemental is. My understanding of the answer is as follows. There exist several planes or levels of subtlety of matter-energy, of which the physical plane is the most dense.

Immediately above the physical plane comes the astral or emotional plane, next the mental plane, and so forth. The physical plane is that of which all we can see, feel and touch around us is comprised. Physical eyes can only see the physical plane, so that the higher planes are invisible unless observed clairvoyantly. The physical plane itself is, however, comprised of seven sub-planes, each of a different level or subtlety of matter-energy. The densest sub-plane of the physical plane is that of solid matter. In ascending order, matter of the next sub-plane of lesser density is that of fluids. Still more subtle than fluids are gasses, which are the material of the third sub-plane. Beyond this, normal human senses cannot discern, so that four of the seven sub-planes of the physical plane are invisible to and unsuspected by most people, even though they are still made up of physical particles of a kind. These four sub-planes are what the alchemists were sometimes referring to, in ascending order, as Earth, Water, Air and Fire.

From this it can be grasped that elementals actually inhabit physical forms! But these physical forms are of a more tenuous nature than ours. Solid matter, fluids and gasses are composed of atoms, and atoms are composed of protons, electrons and neutrons. When protons, electrons and neutrons come together to form atoms, then we have those constituent elements of the physical world which we are familiar with, and which combine to form every solid, every fluid, and every gas. But if such particles do not combine in the form of atoms, they still exist, yet are too tenuous to be perceived by us. Such free particles are known in physics as plasma. I believe it is such plasma that high-voltage or Kirlian photography captures on photographic plates. And it is such plasma that goes to make up the 'bodies' of elemental beings.

This is very interesting for a number of reasons. For one thing, full clairvoyance may not always be necessary in order to see elementals, and a number of clairvoyants actually attest to this fact. Physical human bodies, including the eyes, exist at all seven of the physical sub-planes. Therefore, since the forms of elementals are composed of physical particles, albeit in the state of plasma, it follows that those levels of vibration of our eyes which also exist in these higher sub-planes of the physical plane should be able to see elementals under the right conditions.

This partly explains why many people in the chapters that follow speak of literally 'seeing' elementals with their eyes. They were seeing with the "higher" aspects of their physical eyes.

Furthermore, if elementals actually inhabit subtle but nevertheless 'physical' bodies, this explains why they are the tenders of nature. It explains how they are able to make plants grow, to move the wind or the waves, to create fire, or to determine the shape of a tree. How would a totally spiritual being be able to interact with nature so closely and intimately? Such a being does not easily have any point of contact with the physical world.

But elementals can and do interact with the physical world. Because they live at the same level as the higher sub-planes of the physical forms of flowers, vegetables and trees, elementals can nourish plant-life with semi-physical energy or chi. They can literally touch the air to move it, and can govern the activities of all water and all fire. They are also intimately associated with our own bodily health. And since the smallest elementals are said to be extremely tiny and even microscopic, what of such Kirlian photographs as most of us have seen, of leaves or of human hands, which depict coloured globules of moving light which are so apparent, emerging from the form, travelling around it, and entering into it again? *Can it be that these are actually photographs of the tiniest of elementals or fairies?* And could there be a way to adapt Kirlian photography or something similar in order to photograph larger elementals - yes, literally to be *photographing fairies?*

Finally, it is necessary to explain where elementals fit into the cosmic scheme of things as compared to, say, the human kingdom and the angelic kingdom. Sometimes people confuse the more classically fairy-like elemental with angels, but the human, angelic and elemental kingdoms are distinct. The number 3 is of profound importance in shaping the entire universe, and the nature of all existence. Every religion stresses the importance of phenomena occurring in threes, such as in the Trinity of Christianity. In Hinduism the Trinity is Brahma, Vishnu and Shiva. Atoms themselves are composed of three smaller kinds of particles that correspond to the spiritual trinity: protons (charged positively), electrons (charged negatively) and neutrons (charged neutrally). Kundalini energy, present on the spinal altar of man and woman, and which is the evolutionary force in all nature, has the three aspects of sushumna, ida and pingala. So it is that these three evolutionary forces are also represented in the three fundamental evolutionary lifewaves present throughout cosmos: the kingdoms of humans, angels, and elementals.

All three evolutionary kingdoms are divinely intended to be at-one and in communion with each other. But humanity has for the most part been out of touch with the kingdoms of the angels and of the elementals for many a century. The time is now at hand to correct this. In fact the state of planet earth, and the spiritual state of humanity as a whole, are now so dire that it is essential to get back in touch with the reality of the angels and the elementals. For they have the answers to all life's problems, the answers and the knowledge that people so long for deep within their hearts. In recent years there has been a great deal of increased interest in angels. And it is now vital that there be a resurgence of interest in and co-operation with nature's hidden gardeners, the blessed beings of the elements. That we may cultivate an enhanced awareness of their ever-present reality, that we may become more knowledgeable of them, and that we may learn to work with them, and to love to do so: to this cause is this book dedicated.

2

Faíríes Have Enhanced My Lífe

Claire Nahmad *lives near Scunthorpe, North Lincolnshire. The author of several books on nature spirits, Claire is the mother of Rebecca, a music graduate in her twenties. Claire has had a number of fairy experiences, the first when she was seven and on a family holiday in Wales*:

We had stopped for a picnic at the foot of a mountain and my brother and I went off to play but got separated. I became totally lost and, being frightened, I made a subconscious plea for help from the other world and, suddenly, I heard voices calling. I followed the sound, thinking it was my parents, and, true enough, I turned a corner, saw them at a distance and was able to run into my dad's arms. When I reached them, I asked if they had called me and they said: "No" - they hadn't known I was lost.

When I first saw fairies I was sixteen and still at school. It happened on the shores of a little lake near my home in Haxey, Lincolnshire, when I was out with my boyfriend, Ken. It was twilight and, although I didn't realise it then, fairies are twilight people; they exist in that sphere of consciousness between being wide-awake and totally oblivious. We used to go to the lake in the early evening and stay until dark. That summer we kept noticing an electric charge building up in the atmosphere.

Then one evening all kinds of things started to happen, there was a tremendous beating of wings, though no birds were there, and a powerful wind shook the bushes, even though everything else remained still. As the twilight deepened, small figures appeared and danced on the water. They were flowing, graceful, and although the light didn't allow us to see colours, I had the impression that they were silver, blue and grey. They seemed eager to make contact, remaining in mental communion with us as they floated away down the lake. My boyfriend saw them too, and I think the experience led to the break-up of our relationship because of a fundamental disagreement over what it meant. Ken felt we were being honoured by supernatural powers because we were special and in some way deserved it. I said that we weren't special, it was just that the fairies had *allowed* us to see them and we should feel privileged rather than deserving. He was excited and full-of-himself but I felt in awe of them, I was humbled. There was such a difference in attitude that we split up.

I realised then that there are other beings on earth who are beautiful, close by and who are always going to be there to help, guide and make life better. It was such a subtle but undeniable experience that I never once thought it was just my imagination - it didn't have the wishy-washy element of fantasy. It was very clear. I had always been aware that there were more dimensions to life than those I could see and hear, but it was only gradually that I realised other people didn't share my belief. That was quite a shock.

Fairies have enhanced my life and although the actual meetings have been few, I feel they talk to me mentally. Just being in contact with fairies, meditating and feeling them talking to me in quiet places is comforting. Fairies and human beings are made for each other, they are meant to interact. And when they do something very remarkable takes place.

3

I Saw the Mountain Open

Hazel Raven *is a therapist who lives in Manchester with her husband Graham. In interview by a national newspaper she had this to say*:

Have you ever seen a hummingbird? They move so fast that you can't see their wings. That's how fairies move - very, very fast. They are also the same size as hummingbirds - around 3 inches long.

I first became aware of fairies as a child. I saw incredible lights, which would slow down like a fluttering butterfly, before realising they were tiny figures - pretty little things with wings like gossamer. Whenever I'm out in the woods I see them - and not just in this country. I spend time in America and they have fairies, too.

My first sighting as a child was probably the most memorable. I was in Wales, sitting on the grass looking at Snowdon, when I saw the mountain open and lots of little people coming out - fairies. I ran excitedly to tell my parents, who were quite cross, saying this kind of thing doesn't happen. But it does. As an adult I was in the Rockies and the mountains opened there, too. Sparkling lights poured out and became the tiny forms. It felt incredibly beautiful, gentle, loving and peaceful.

I tend to see fairies early morning or evening in places where people don't go so much, or where gardens have been turned over to nature, like mine. Everybody has the potential to see them, or at least to be aware they are there. It's a question of tuning in. People tend to see lights first because fairies don't instantly reveal their whole selves. I think they help human beings get in touch with the part of them they've lost - the child part, the purity.

4

Did I See Him?

The following account is from a farmer's wife near Timberscombe, and took place in 1962. She recounted it to folklorist R.L. Tongue, who published it in a booklet of Somerset folklore three years after the event.

I've never seen a ghost, but I *did* see a fairy. It was on the Berkshire Downs, and we'd lost our way, and didn't know what track to take. When I looked round, there was a small man in green standing at my elbow. He had a round smiling face, and he said, "You take that one; you'll be all right." Then he didn't disappear, but he just wasn't there anymore. Did I see him? Or didn't I?

5

I Was Surrounded By Life

Brian Froud, *aged 50 in 1997, is an artist and illustrator. He lives at Chagford, near Exeter, with his wife Wendy, 45, and son Toby, 13. Brian says that "unfortunately" fairies have taken over his creative life. His pictures come intuitively, take a long time, and while some are of the more typical depiction of fairies, being pretty and winged, others are rather lumpy and grotesque.*

Doesn't everyone believe in fairies? When I went to college to study graphic design I came across a book by Arthur Rackham which showed wonderful trees with faces. They reminded me that, as a child, I went to a country school surrounded by woods. Suddenly there was the recognition of what I felt as a child--that I was surrounded by life. That started my interest in fairies. I did a lot of research and began to paint them.

Like me, my son was aware of fairies when he was quite young. He complained about a blue thing that shot through his room and pink boys under his bed. Toby was quite convinced he had seen these pink boys. He said they were little gnome figures who were pulling faces and making him cry. I got a psychic friend to frighten them and banish them to the bottom of the garden. Once they were back down there, everything was fine.

Children tend to be able to see fairies more than adults because the rational mind takes over and we lose our ability to see them. The concept of fairies most of us have is of pretty creatures with gossamer wings and gauzy dresses. My [painted] fairies range from that to strange, bog-eyed ones. I also paint pictures of pure light, which is the energy of the fairy and the way they actually are. They just form themselves into more recognisable images so we can understand them. They're the hidden agencies of nature and the energies underneath it all.

Fairies don't always have wings, and the wings are not used to fly. Fairies can move through the air, but they don't actually flap with wings. It is all the forces, the energy flowing through their bodies and out of the back, which create the wing shape.

I believe that as well as being in woods, fairies are also in urban areas. You're just as likely to see one in the middle of Trafalgar Square.

They like people who are open to them and they will reveal themselves when they're so inclined.

6

Little Men in Procession

Maggie O'Neill, *a friend of mine, is in her thirties and lives in East London. She is of Irish origin but was living in Clapton, London when the following experience occurred when she was 5 or 6 years old. She still wonders how she would react if she saw the same thing again today as an adult.*

I would be alone in bed at night. But I am certain that I was awake. Little men would march in a procession, in a line, across my bed, along the floor, and even up the wall. There were hundreds, *millions* of them. I'd say they averaged four inches tall, but they were all in fact of various heights, and there were fat ones and thin ones. This happened to me five or six times within a year. Each time it happened I was terrified, because I didn't know what I was seeing. I would cry out very loud, and when my mother came in the little men would disappear.

For years after this I suffered from very bad fear of spiders, arachnophobia. It is hard to say whether I had this before I saw the little men, but it is possible this fear was actually brought on by what I saw. Over the years the arachnophobia receded.

7

Cellini's Salamander

Benvenuto Cellini *was in his day (1500-1571) one of Europe's greatest artisans in sculpture, goldsmithry, portraiture, and the stamping of coins and medals. He apprenticed as a metal worker at an early age in the studio of the Florentine goldsmith Andrea di Sandro Marcone, was later "stamp master" at the papal mint in Rome, and is famed for his marble figures of "Apollo" and "Hyacinth" (1546), "Narcissus" (1546-7) and others. The Kunsthistoriches Museum of Vienna holds the salt-cellar he crafted in gold for King Francis I, considered the supreme example of Renaissance goldsmithry. Cellini also experienced an extremely adventurous and dangerous life, which he recounted in an autobiography written between 1558 and 1562. And in this autobiography, in plain matter-of-fact language, this famous figure tells of his seeing a salamander (an elemental or fairy of the fire element).*

When I was about five years old my father happened to be in a basement-chamber of our house, where they had been working, and where a good fire of oak-logs was still burning; he had a vial in his hand and was playing and singing alone before the fire. The weather was very cold. Happening to look into the fire he spied in the middle of those most burning flames a little creature like a lizard, that was sporting in the core of the intensest coals. [Modern sears report many types of salamanders, the higher orders being huge and graceful,

but even in the twentieth century Dora van Gelder reported that the lowest forms "look like insects, or lizards, or beetles" and are called into being (or called into coming near) by ordinary small fires.] Becoming instantly aware of what the thing was, he had my sister and me called, and pointing it out to us children, gave me a great box on the ears which caused me to howl and weep with all my might. Then he pacified me good-humouredly and spoke as follows:

"My dear little boy, I am not striking you for any wrong that you have done, but only to make you remember that that lizard which you see in the fire is a salamander, a creature which has never been seen by anyone of whom we have credible information." So saying he kissed me and gave me some pieces of money.

8

A Fairy Funeral

William Blake *(1757-1827), the quite unique poet, painter and mystic, mentions fairy folk in several of his poems, but Blake's poetry is extremely allegorical, and here his fairies, just as the other beings which inhabit his poetry, seem to represent qualities or temptations which are difficult to fathom. However in his private letters and conversations he spoke of ordinary daily life, and then he mentioned fairies plainly, as a countryman might do. Indeed he seemed to believe that he actually saw them. This is one conversation Blake is reported to have had.*

"Did you ever see a fairy's funeral, madam?" he said to a lady who happened to sit next to him.

"Never, Sir!" replied the lady.

"I have," said Blake, "but not before last night." And he went on to tell how, in his garden, he had seen "a procession of creatures of the size and colour of green and grey grasshoppers, bearing a body laid out on a rose-leaf, which they buried with songs, and then disappeared".

9

Dancing in a Ring

Whether the experience of seeing nature spirits happened in modern times or in ancient times, people have not always been willing to speak openly of what they have witnessed for fear of ridicule. For this reason it is difficult to know just how many, or what percentage, of the population of any nation may believe they have seen such beings. The following is such an account, which came to light only because the man involved was a personal friend of Walter Gill, who was compiling books on the Isle of Man including its folklore. This friend had known Gill for thirty-five years, and was originally from Liverpool. But on a date which, from the publication date and the account itself, we can estimate to have been around 1897, he saw that which he had never expected to see and had previously never even believed in.

About 34 years ago, when he was 23, at 10 a.m. of a brilliantly sunny summer morning he was walking on the short grass below the debris at the west side of the Glen Aldyn slate-quarries, which lie far above the inhabited part of the Glen. Here he came to a sudden stop to avoid stepping on something alive between two and three yards in front of him. It was five little creatures dancing in a ring, hand in hand. They stood a foot or 18 inches high and were greyish in colour like fungus, their bodies seeming to be swollen in front, their limbs and eyes clearly distinguishable, and their heads moving as they danced. He speaks of them as 'little men' because they gave him a strong impression of being of

the male sex. After he had watched them for a short time they vanished from his sight, and there was nothing there but the grass. Thinking his eyes or brain might have played him a trick, he went to the same spot a couple of mornings later, and there they were again, just as before. He has hardly ever spoken of it to anyone for fear of ridicule.

10

The Grace of Her Exit

Some people's experiences are one-offs for them, and therefore may leave them forever after in a state of bewilderment or wonder. Other individuals, however, who could clearly be categorised as clairvoyant to a greater or lesser degree, have a number of such encounters and may come to accept them as a part of their normal life. Such a person was obviously the Scotsman Struan Robertson, who gave the following report in 1936.

The first fairy I met was alone upon a hillside near Aberfoyle, where Robert Kirk wrote his *Commonwealth of Fairies*. She was very friendly, beckoned me to follow her, and eventually showed me the most wonderful of sights. [Unfortunately Robertson does not expand on this. It would have been interesting to know exactly what he saw.]

One afternoon in Arran I saw ten fairies playing out and in among gorse bushes and round about the grazing sheep. The sheep were quite undisturbed except that if a fairy went too near one of then it would trot off for a few yards.

Wandering in a wood in Arran one morning I heard the silvery plangent accents of fairies, and following the sounds I saw quite a clan of them hurrying along a green footpath. They seemed angry about something. Observing me, they chattered loudly, scattered as one sees a flock of excited sparrows scattering, increased their speed and fled.

Tramping near Lock Rannock I was attracted by tuneful tones coming from clumps of rhododendrons, and advancing cautiously beheld the most beautiful dancing. I was too interested to count the number of fairies, concentrating upon how close I could get.

When I was within ten paces of them one sighted me, and alarming the dancers she shepherded them in among the bushes. I shall never forget the glance she gave me as she disappeared, and the gesture, the grace of her exit, I have seen approached only in the incomparable Pavlova herself.

11

'I Want To Show You Something'

Staying with Scotland, here is an account from the Isle of Skye sent to the great collector of fairy folklore Katherine Briggs in 1958 by Mona Smith, the wife of an Edinburgh minister. The account raises a puzzling and abiding question. When a number of people together see nature spirits, does this mean that one of them, being clairvoyant, is unconsciously and temporarily passing this ability on to those immediately near them? Or are there multiple witnesses because the nature spirits have at that place and time become sufficiently solid and visible for absolutely anybody to see, and perhaps to photograph them?

In the darkening of an Autumn evening over eighty years ago a little boy in the Isle of Skye was awaiting the return of his mother from a visit to an ailing neighbour.

He and an elder sister had been left with their grandmother while their mother was on her errand of mercy. Another little boy had joined them, and all three had played happily during the afternoon. Their own home was some distance from their grandmother's - just too far for little ones unaccompanied. Presently there came to call on the grand-mother an elderly woman from the village, one whom the children knew well and whom they liked. Probably by this time they were becoming a little tired and cross, and their old friend was trying to amuse them. Suddenly she said, 'Come with me, I want to show you something.'

They all took hands and went out into the gloaming, and down the path by the side of the burn. Then the old lady stopped, and said: 'Look, do you see them?' And there, on the hill-side, all dressed in green, were fairies dancing in a ring round a fire.

The children were simply enchanted by what they saw, and one can imagine their excitement, and the wonderful story they had to tell their mother on her return.

Next morning they rushed out to look for the ashes of the fairy fire, but there was nothing to be seen.

That little boy was my father, and as children my brother and sisters and I were never tired of hearing this story. My aunt too, when she came to visit us, would corroborate the tale. And I have passed it on to mine, and have shown them the green, grassy mound 'where Papa saw the fairies.'

Two years ago, and for the first time, I met the third child, now an old man, and he could recall, as vividly and clearly as if it were yesterday, all the details of that wonderful evening. For those who might like to try and explain this experience, I must tell them that the old lady was credited with the second sight.

12

A Much-Haunted Terrain

It is not only particular people who tend to see nature spirits, but also there are particular places in which it seems they are much more frequently encountered. The clairvoyant Marko Pogacnik, from whom we shall have an account later, calls these "nature temples". According to Pogacnik, when humanity build over these areas remorselessly it does great damage to the spiritual ecosystem and energy flow. On the other hand, he says, humanity often subconsciously attunes to such areas, and builds around them, and he cites Kensington Gardens in London as an example, calling it "a huge, intact nature temple". In old folklore there exists numerous tales of nature spirits behaving in an annoying, mischievous and occasionally frightening manner. These two phenomena may well sometimes be linked, the nature spirits being mischievous in order to discourage building or even agriculture upon an existing nature temple. This is one possibility behind the next account, in which **S. John Saunders**, *in 1986, described the experiences of himself and others in Boxted, Sussex.*

Barely four miles from my rural Essex home is the village of Broxted (Brocks'-Head), site of an ancient pagan shrine, where tractors grind to a shuddering halt, crops unaccountably wither, and 'gnomes' have been sighted *in broad daylight*. A former vicar once attempted a scientific probe, but was balked by fear and superstition.

I first happened across this spectral landscape in 1964, since which time I have explored the area by car, bicycle and on foot. I have experienced an unaccountable skid on my bike (something unseen tried to throw me off), been stuck in the lanes in a car which refused to budge, and sensed an evil presence whilst bathing in an adjacent stream. In 1966 I led an expedition to the site which included Madame Clara, a noted East London clairvoyant. She described visions of dwarfs, said that she could hear 'hammering noises' and the beat of wings, and became very distressed. The visit had to be abandoned.

Since that time I have talked long and searchingly to the late owner and present manager of Coldarbour Farm, centre of the disturbances. I have been told of three separate bulldozers which recently stalled on the site. Of a watertank on its way to the farmhouse which inexplicably overturned. Of vanishing tools and enigmatic voices heard at dusk, and other dark happenings which continue to this day. Other residents speak of one Bob Wallis who until recently ran a smallholding in the area and would constantly complain of being watched and mocked by the little people whilst at his labours. And two cottagers - now dead - swore that goblin-esque figures would suddenly appear in their homes. Indeed one elderly witness still tells of 'they little men' who would waylay people at night if they supped too long at the local inn!

In September 1976, while being interviewed by me for a television feature, Keith Foster, a young tractor-driver living on the site, spoke of the day three years earlier when while ploughing the fields a cutting block broke, was repaired hastily, upon which two bolts snapped and a combine harvester mysteriously stalled. He recounted also the occasion in 1974 when he and his sister twice saw a diminutive hooded figure in the near distance, which 'evaporated' as they watched.

During the late autumn of 1978 I paid another visit to the area on a bicycle, and came across a huddle of men struggling with a recalcitrant car on the ancient trackway skirting Coldarbour Farm. A dog was howling, and the sky suddenly became black with scudding clouds although the sun was shining elsewhere. On the way back my gears packed up and I walked the rest of the way home. Such happenings are commonplace in this much-haunted terrain.

34

13

Healed By a Tiny Man in Green

I have mentioned that Kensington Gardens in London is a huge nature temple according to clairvoyant observation. I cannot say whether Regents Park of the same city (which is near to where I now write) is the same, but we might expect such an area of greenery to be more comfortable to nature spirits than the concrete and noisy roads that surround it. Thus, for a London dweller, it is presumably a more likely place to meet one of the 'little' folk. And so it proved for a clergyman's widow who was also a friend of folklorist Katherine Briggs. As Briggs recounts what this friend told her:

She suffers from an injured foot, and one day she was sitting on a seat in Regents Park, wondering how she would find strength and courage to go home. Suddenly she saw a tiny man in green, who looked at her very kindly and said, 'Go home. We promise that your foot shan't pain you tonight.' Then he disappeared, but the pain, which had been considerable, was quite gone. She walked home easily, and all that night she slept painlessly. On another occasion she had seen a group of fairies dressed in flowers dancing together on one side of the flower-beds, but this had only been a momentary glimpse and she had heard nothing.

14

The Fairy of the Rose

Cynthia Montefiore *of Somerset has written of two sightings she had during her childhood. What she saw is most reminiscent of the descriptions given by the two girls who claimed to have seen the famed Cottingley fairies (whatever the truth of the case), and whose tale was retold in the movie* Fairy Tale. *Mrs Montefiore's first sighting does indeed sound like something right out of that film, though she wrote of the event in 1977.*

I was in the garden with my mother at her home when this occurred. Mother wanted to show me the correct way to take cuttings from rose trees. She stood behind the finest rose tree we had with a pair of scissors in her hand, while I stood in front of it. Thus we faced one another with the rose tree between us.

Suddenly Mother put a finger to her lips to indicate silence and then pointed to one of the blooms. With astonishment I saw what she was seeing - a little figure about six inches high, in the perfect shape of a woman and with brilliantly coloured diaphanous wings resembling those of a dragonfly.

The figure held a little wand and was pointing at the heart of the rose. At the tip of the wand there was a little light, like a star. The figure's limbs were very pale pink and visible through her clothes. She had long silvery hair which resembled an aura. She hovered near the rose for a least two

minutes, her wings vibrating rapidly like those of a hummingbird and then she disappeared.

'You saw that, didn't you?' asked my mother. I nodded and
we both went back to the house astonished and enriched by
our mutual experience and having forgotten entirely the
rose-cutting.

Perhaps the most surprising aspect of the experience was the
way in which the little creature we both saw corresponded in
practically every detail to the archetypal fairy of folklore and
nursery stories. I know now that these descriptions are
firmly founded on reality.

This was proved to me once again by a second experience I
had when I was alone in the same garden. I was sitting
reading under a tree when my eye was caught by a sudden
movement in front of me. A little figure, about 18 inches tall,
ran from the lawn on my left, across a path and onto another
lawn, finally disappearing under a young fir tree. The
sturdily build figure seemed to be dressed in a brown one-
piece suit. I was not able to see the face because it was
turned away from me. I immediately jumped up to invest-
igate the area around the fir tree but there was no longer any
sign of this gnome.

Not long after this episode a man friend of the family, who
was obliging my mother by digging in the vegetable garden,
saw the selfsame gnome and described it to me.

15

The Father of Modern Hermetics

Paracelsus *(1493-1541, born in Switzerland as Theophrastus Bombastus von Hohenheim) was an alchemist and hermetic philosopher who travelled widely, and it was he who became the first westerner in comparatively recent times to describe the world of nature spirits in some detail and as an occult scientist. In Paracelsus' case, rather than to simply quote him, I feel it would be useful to comment a little on his statements as well.*

To Paracelsus the nature kingdoms were not folklore, but absolute fact. Adding his own discoveries to what he learned from the Oriental sages (probably Brahmanic) whom he met, Paracelsus became the first European to describe the four relatively distinct kingdoms of salamanders, sylphs, undines and gnomes.

It was Paracelsus who coined the term "elemental", for these beings who dwell within the four elements of fire, air, water and earth. Paracelsus remains the father, as it were, of all modern clairvoyants, researchers, writers and hermetics who study and work with the nature kingdoms.

It is clear that what Paracelsus had to say was new and controversial to many of his own time. "Neither let me raise scandal," he wrote, "upon this my writing of Philosophy, but first rather let him well peruse and ponder every word; and then it will appeare from whom I spake, and whether I have this knowledge from the Devil, or from the experience of the pure light of nature."

So where are the elementals? Why can we not see them, or where have they gone? Paracelsus addressed this question: "In old times many of them have been found and heard amongst men, but now they cease; but no man hitherto hath known, or could give a reason of their severing and separation, seeing they always have been esteemed to be Immortal creatures; because no man could certainly be able to know or finde out their death, or could consider any cause of their absence: neither could any man for a long time be able to know what they now are, or whence they proceeded, or whether they wander, or what gift or office they have. Many do suppose that where they bring any benefits or good to men, that they are Angels, or good and familiar Spirits, sent to men from God... for oftentimes they bring to men very many good offices and benefits, and do undertake and sustaine many hard labours for them. Others believe that they will not be seen by us, because that when a man seeth them, he cryeth out, so that they vanish away."

Paracelsus, however, was able to tell where the elementals resided. He wrote of his belief, or rather his knowledge, that the four primary elements recognized by the ancients, and known to the alchemists, were actual substances, but at a more subtle or vapourous level of existence than their tangible counterparts. Water, for example, of the visible, tangible kind which we drink and wash in, also had a less tangible or ethereal counterpart which was beyond normal human perceptive abilities - the Water of the ancients and of the hermetics. And so on for earth, air and fire. Thus, concerning the elementals:

"They live in the four elements: the Nymphae in the element of water, the Sylphes in that of the air, the Pigmies in the earth, and the Salamanders in fire. They are also called Undinae, Sylvestres, Gnomi, Vulcani, &c. Each species moves only in the element to which it belongs, and neither of them can go out of its appropriate element, which is to them as the air is to us, or the water to fishes; and none of them can live in the element belonging to another class. To each elemental being the element in which it lives is transparent, invisible and respirable, as the atmosphere is to ourselves."

The elementals' very bodies, Paracelsus explained, are made up of the substance or element in which they reside, so that their forms are very different to the corporeal bodies of men descended from Adam. "Yet the Elementals are not spirits, because they have flesh, blood and bones [this is not strictly true, but they do have form, and 'organs' more accurately thought of as being energy centres - D.T.]; they live and propagate offspring; they eat and talk, act and sleep, etc., and consequently they cannot be properly called 'spirits'. They are beings occupying a place between men and spirits, resembling men and spirits, resembling men and women in their organisation and form, and resembling spirits in the rapidity of their locomotion."

That elementals are not spirits, angels or gods Paracelsus was at pains to repeat and make quite clear. In fact, his words ring as though this point was very much stressed to him by his own teachers. For example, in his description of the gnomes: "Under the earth do wander half-men, which possess all temporal things, which they want or are delighted with; they are Vulgarly called "Gnomi", or Inhabiters of the Mountains... They are not Spirits, as others are, but are compared unto them, for the Similitude of their Arts and Industry, which are common to them with the Spirits: they have flesh and blood as men, which no real Spirit has... we are to know that these are not to be reputed Spirits, but like to Spirits; but if they are or shall be called Spirits, they aught to be called earthly Spirits, because they have their Chaos and habitation under the earth."

Furthermore, unlike spirits or gods, the elementals are not immortal. As our own bodies are formed and later disintegrate "ashes to ashes, dust to dust", so too the elementals are formed out of the element of their own particular kingdom, but the form thus created does not endure forever. At death, said Paracelsus, the substance of their bodies merely merges back into all the rest of the substance of that element.

No individual consciousness is preserved after death, for their entire being is composed of the elemental substance of their particular kingdom. This is a more refined substance than that of our world, but it is not 'Spirit'; elementals possess no Spirit or Higher Self. However, little wear and tear is incurred by their activities, since their bodies are more energetic than material, so that many live to a great age. According to Paracelsus the average life-span of an elemental is between three hundred and a thousand years, gnomes being the shortest-lived and sylphs and salamanders the longest.

And then, amid his descriptive passages about elementals, Paracelsus turns once more to the subject of their role or place in the cosmic scheme of things, and how humanity should regard them. His point of emphasis is still worth making today, for in today's thriving alternative culture there still is found the tendency to be in awe of nature spirits (which is a form of worship), simply because they are of a different plane of existence. It is worth noting that nature spirits, especially those less developed, are often in awe of humanity, for they frequently do not possess our gift of intellect, our ability to make free-will decisions, or our potential for immortality by growing in spirituality through the rounds of reincarnation. This is my twenty-first century way of putting it; but in Paracelsus's own words on the elementals:

"These are they of whom God Almighty admonisheth us in that Commandment of the First Tablet, saying, that we shall not have any other Gods but him, neither in the waters (where the "Nymphs" are understood) nor under the Earth, (by which he meaneth "Sylphes" or "Pygmies")."

In that sentence Paracelsus proves himself to be the first person ever able to correctly understand or rationally explain this part of Exodus 20:3-5, apart from the fact that we should not worship idols. It is not that Paracelsus believed exclusively in a transcendent, monotheistic God. He recognized the immanence of Spirit in all men, and throughout all nature. (As an alchemist he certainly did this.) But he saw that there is truth in both points of view, and in others beside. Paracelsus, father of the modern interest in nature spirits, was an animist, a monotheist, and a pantheist all in one.

16

Into the Real World of Fairies

In the twentieth century a number of individuals developed clairvoyant abilities probably even in excess of those of Paracelsus, and were all associated with the Theosophical Society. Among these was **Dora Van Gelder,** *who was able to watch and interact with gnomes, undines, sylphs and salamanders from early childhood. In the 1920s she wrote a charming book-length manuscript describing the nature kingdom in extensive detail. Though not published until as late as 1977, this is in fact among the small handful of very best books on the subject, and I would recommend it to all. (Though after the twenties she married,* The Real World of Fairies *is published under her maiden name as above.) Here are two extracts, one of a childhood experience in Australia which tells much about how the nature spirits are organised, being overseen by angel devas, and one extract which describes the typical different kinds of elementals likely to be found in any garden. Reading this helps us to know what kinds of beings are present in our garden, and with whom we can interact, even if we cannot quite see them.*

The relation we could all have with fairies can be illustrated by one incident. Many years ago some friends celebrated my fourteenth birthday with a picnic at National Park in Australia. In the party there were others who could see, and as we sat on the bank of the main stream in the park we remarked the numbers of curious and friendly fairies peering at us from the bush. This was our first visit to the park, and the wealth of fairy life led us to get in touch with the angel of the area. He proved to be a remarkable character, of great stature, and with an air of power and determination. He was accustomed to rule and carry out his plans, but all in a way imbued with great kindness. He had been attracted to one member of our party who wore a jewelled cross, everywhere a symbol of power, and in this case a jewel with a very special radiation of light.

So the angel remarked on it, and said as much to us. He was interested to find that we were capable of talking to him and seeing fairies. He wanted to know all about the cross and even expressed a desire to have something of a similar nature and asked us if we could not get him one. We were of course curious to know what made him want such a thing and he explained. It appeared that he was ensouling this great valley and that he had a scheme for it. He had divided the valley into three parts, and in each place he wanted a different influence to be maintained. To this end he placed in and along the lower basin, which was tidal, a certain kind of fairy, which is to be found in the sea, and also an inter-mediate sort which inhabits brackish waters; and higher, on the land, some gnomes and some emerald green fairies. Then, above this, there was a weir and quiet water, and in and around this he had established particularly fine sweet water fairies, a light powder or turquoise blue in colour, very human looking, and on the surrounding land many sky blue woods fairies and many splendid little butterfly fellows.

Still higher up the stream, where it grew inaccessible and wild, he kept up a third atmosphere, with fairies of a kind more aloof from humanity. He wanted a jewel cross put somewhere in the central section of the valley to establish a centre point of influence for that part of the area. We were interested in all this, and promised to get him a cross if possible. He was exceedingly pleased with the idea, and most grateful.

Our party sang songs, as one does on such occasions, and this brought fairies from all over the place, the angel looking on all the time. They crowded round and were amazed to find people who could talk to them and who appreciated what they were about. When it came time to go, they begged us to come back again.

In due course, a friend and I returned on the day we had appointed to give the angel the cross, but without it. As soon as we came down to the place, in fact, before we really got there, the angel's first question was, "Have you got the cross?" I explained that we hadn't, because it was not yet ready. At this he was extremely disappointed and said one really should keep one's promises, once given, and that such things do not happen in the angelic kingdom. That slips occur in our material world did not count with him. But we stayed and had an enjoyable time making friends with several pleasant fairies who were delighted to talk to us. For the angel's plan included the helping of human beings, who came there in thousands on holidays. He wanted to give them some feeling of rest, and the fairies were told to be as kind as possible to visitors and to try to understand them. So they were always curious about human doings and had more than the usual interest in finding a couple of human beings willing to talk to them and able to explain the vagaries of human behaviour. Some points were mysterious to them. For example, football was played there by holiday crowds. The fairies could understand the running, but did not make out why the ball was an object of such fierce pursuit. We never managed to make this clear, except to convey that it was a game. We promised the angel that we would come back and bring the cross without fail.

It was finally ready, and we took it down to the Park. The angel explained to us where he wanted it put, but after walking a couple of miles and finding the place, we discovered it was particularly horrible, with a gruesomely unpleasant atmosphere due, I am bound to admit, to human misdeeds. We appealed to the angel and he said that he wanted the cross in this unpleasant place just because it was so unsavoury. He hoped the radiations of the jewel would set it right. We begged him not to insist on that, but to select a lovely spot where it would do its work with help from the surroundings. He called another angel into the discussion and finally it was decided to put the cross in a spot of great beauty, and more centrally located. Accordingly it was concealed there and at once the angel called all the fairies of the valley to the place. Thousands came to join the hundreds who already had been watching the business with great curiosity. The angel explained the purpose of the jewels and he held then and there a ceremony to celebrate the acquisition. The fairies passed around a circle in a slow winding dance, delightful in this addition to the beauties of the park. They were told by the angel to come there constantly and bathe in the radiations of the jewels, and so carry the new influence about the park.

Such an episode is of course rare, but fairies in gardens everyday are in touch with human beings. Generally when people come into a garden they know nothing about the fairies there. The fairies know, however, but as there is no human response, they go about their own business.

They always take notice of children and especially of quite small ones, as they have much affection for children, who are in the human order the nearest thing to them. If, however, we walk in a garden even without seeing the fairies but imagine their presence, we are sure to get into touch with them, especially when we stop to admire the flowers.

Among the beings who live on the surface of the land, one of the most important sections is associated with the woods and gardens, and includes the spirits of trees. Perhaps the best way to convey the special qualities of these fairies is to describe members of each natural division: those of the garden and those of the forest.

There are several types of garden fairies. The smallest of these has the proportions of a candle, and is rather feminine in appearance. They are from nine inches to a foot tall with a head a couple of inches long and a human face where the flame would be, but in colouring the body is bright apple-green or yellow and the face tan. They possess hands and arms, in proportion, and just suggestions of short legs and feet. This particular fairy seems to deal with little plants that grow in borders, such as lobelia, and alyssum and masses of small plants in groups. These beings do not respond very much to creatures or events outside their immediate world; they are rather primitive in their reactions, though capable of feeling both affection and jealousy for their plants and for one another. They are avid for new sensations, for that is the way they learn. Groups of three and four are to be seen drifting about any pleasant attractive garden.

Then, among the tulips and similar flowers there is a type that is about a foot tall, much more human in appearance than "candle" fairies, but still rather like human shadows, having the outline without the substance-form of faint purple light. Some of them have delicate long faces, rather like a faun's. One would never mistake them for human beings, not only because of their diminutive stature, but because they are such a quaint caricature, and because they look so tenuous. Their limbs are human enough, but frequent imperfection of hands and feet appear. They have a variety of fingers and toes, and some of their hands look more like the paws of a kitten. Around them is a kind of diaphanous matter that seems phosphorescent, in beautiful shades of rose and light purple.

In this particular garden that I am describing there were some lovely beds of pansies. About them floated some equally lovely and delicate beings which remind one of butterflies, and are short-lived. They are tiny things, only a few inches tall, having faces much like the pansy itself. The body is very like that of a butterfly or dragonfly - torpedo shaped, and much narrower than the face. The body and head together are perhaps four or five inches long, and of this the face is perhaps an inch. Projecting from the neck and virtually the whole length of the body are two thin wing-like structures, which, however, do not fulfil the function of wings but so far as one can judge, are merely decorative. The face and body are flesh-coloured but tinged with shades of mauve, violet and purple; the wings are similarly coloured, but variegated and brilliant. While I was watching I saw four of these in only a few minutes, moving about the pansies in the window boxes. After all, in the invisible world, just as in the visible, there is a community of life, and fairies are as likely to be wherever there is a bed of flowers as a group of butterflies would be.

We now come to the common garden fairy, in many respects the true, central type of fairy. In fact, he corresponds to what most people mean by fairy when they speak of fairy life... This particular garden has a few rather big specimens, between eighteen inches and two feet tall, and in many ways quite human in appearance. They have a nose, two eyes, a mouth and even ears, and hair rather like wool, usually of a dark brown, like the bark of a tree. The face, like that of all other fairies, has not the same proportions as the human face, because the nose and eyes are spaced more generously. It gives them a permanently surprised look of curiosity. And, indeed, all of these fairies are exceedingly full of curiosity. The lack of eyelids and eyelashes also seems a little strange when first noticed. Their faces are golden brown, and the body, when in repose and not "dressed up", is emerald green, reminding one of the bright green beetles sometimes seen in spring. They have hands and feet quite like ours, although the latter are somewhat more triangular. The whole effect is quite delightful. These fairies were playing among the lilacs in the garden while I observed them. As they have the highest intelligence of all their fellows in the garden, they maintain a sort of supervision over some of the lesser fairies there.

A little pond in the garden had a peculiar kind of creature which, for lack of a better term, I shall call a "spring" fairy. The pond is fed by several springs and in the particular places where this water flowed up from the earth there were strange, long creatures, with something of a jelly-fish appearance; their most definite part is a bluish, dimly featured head, which melts into a bluish body with very little suggestion of neck between. The body fades away into vague, wraithlike tendrils, and continues down into the earth for a considerable distance. These creatures seem to draw their life from within the earth, although they are at the same time definitely connected with water. It is evident that spring water has a kind of vital freshness about it which is the source of their life. These quaint "spring" fairies gener-ally hover at the place where the water emerges from the earth, their heads just out of the water, bobbing slowly up and down.

In a little glazed hot-house I found a few fairies of the butterfly variety, longer by an inch or two than others of their type and more human also, but otherwise much the same. Evidently, after a term of hothouse experience, the butterfly type has become specialised for this special contact with the work of man in forming plants. They are delicate and dainty beings.

17

The Spirit of the Falls

Another individual of striking clairvoyant ability, and who
was also drawn to the Theosophical Society, was Englishman
Geoffrey Hodson. At the same time as Dora Van Gelder, in
the 1920s, Hodson went about a systematic description of
nature spirits as he observed them, as well as other beings
such as angels, archangels, and those men and women who
had transcended the limitations of time, space, karma and
rebirth to become the Masters of Wisdom. In the 1920s he was
still a young man, and the world of nature spirits was quite
new to him, as he had just begun to see these beings. No doubt
with some awe and wonder, he began what can virtually be
called a scientific exploration of this realm. Hodson became,
as it were, a naturalist of the elemental kingdom.

His method was to observe the elementals of whatever
kingdom he saw, which might appear spontaneously during
his everyday life or which he might go out into the countryside
to find, and to tell his wife what he was seeing as he could
best describe it. She wrote down his words. Hodson's best
such book on nature spirits is Fairies at Work and at Play.
From this is taken the following wonderful account of undines
(the water-element elemental kingdom which includes the
mermaids). It is worth reminding the reader here that
elementals consist of a form of matter-energy finer than that
of the world that our physical bodies inhabit. Therefore when
Hodson speaks of undines "deep down" in the water or
springing "out of the solid rock" they are interpenetrating

these materials. In other words, unless she somehow fully materialised, a mermaid plunging into a river would be unobserved by ordinary people and would not make a splash!

The undine belongs to the element of water and, so far as my experience goes, is never to be found away from river, stream and fall. She is definitely female in form and is always nude; she does not usually have wings, and only rarely wears any kind of adornment. Her form, whether diminutive or of human stature, is always entrancingly beautiful, and all her movements are perfect. The waterfall is her favourite haunt, and there she is to be seen disporting herself, generally with a group of her sisters, enjoying to the full the magnetic force of the fall.

Apparently there are periods when the undine retires from the vivid external life in which she is most frequently observed and finds a measure of quiet and repose deep down in the still cool depths of the pools below the falls or in the quieter reaches of the rivers, as well as in lakes and ponds. This life below the waters is in strong and marked contrast to the amazing vividness and joy she manifests amid falling water and sunlit spray.

The three fundamental processes of Nature - absorption, assimilation and discharge - are expressed fully in the outer life of the undine, indeed that life may be said to consist entirely of a continued repetition of those three processes.

Poised amid the spray, or in the centre of the downward rushing torrent, she absorbs, slowly, the magnetism from the sunlight and the fall; as the limit of absorption is reached, she releases, in one dazzling flash of light and colour, the energy with which she is surcharged. At that magical moment of release she experiences an ecstasy and exaltation beyond anything possible to mere mortals dwelling in the prison of the flesh. The expression on the face and particularly in the eyes at that moment is beautiful, I would almost say wonderful, beyond description. The eyes flash with dazzling radiance, the face expresses rapturous joy and a sense of abnormal vitality and power; the whole bearing, the perfect form, and the brilliant splendour of the auric radiance, combine to produce a vision of enchanting loveliness.

This condition is immediately followed by one of dreamy pleasure in which the consciousness is largely withdrawn from the physical plane and centred in emotion. The form becomes vague and indistinct for the time being, until, having assimilated the whole experience, she reappears and repeats the process.

Hodson then describes a Spirit of the Falls in the Lake District, as observed by him in June, 1922:

We are in a bower of bracken and rocks, a veritable Fairyland. The spirit of the falls occasionally appears in the form of a full-sized, nude female of singular beauty. She differs in some characteristics from undines previously observed; she is very much larger than those we have seen before, has a more highly developed intelligence, and is winged. She seems to ensoul the rocks, trees, ferns and mosses, as well as the actual waterfall itself. When first seen, she sprang out of the solid rock - a marvellously beautiful figure - hung poised for a moment in the air and then disappeared. She repeated this process several times, but whether she is visible or not, her presence can always be most distinctly felt.

Her form is a beautiful, pale, rose pink, and suggests a marble statue come to life. The hair is fair and shining, the brow broad, the features beautifully modelled, the eyes large and luminous, and, while their expression has something of the spirit of the wilds, their glance is not unkindly. The wings, which appear to rise from the shoulder blades, are small in proportion to the body, and would surely be inadequate for flight if such had been their purpose; they, too, are of a rosy pink. Even more striking than the form is the rainbow-like aureole which surrounds her, as a halo surrounds the moon. This aura is almost spherical in shape, and consists of evenly arranged, concentric bands of soft yet glorious hues. The colours are too numerous, and in far too rapid movement, for me to detail them, but her aura would seem to contain all the colours of the spectrum in their palest shades, with perhaps rose, green and blue predominating. Some of the bands of colour are outlined with a golden fire and beyond the outer edge a shimmering radiance of pearly white gives an added beauty. Over the head a powerful upward flow of force interpenetrates the aura in a fan-shaped radiation. This appears to come from a point in the middle of the head, where there is a brilliant golden centre, slightly below the level of the eyes, and midway between them. To contact such a creature is an illumination, and I wish that I could find words to describe not only the splendour of her appearance, but the wonderful feeling of exaltation and life incarnate that she gives. The place is vibrant with her life.

A little later.

She now reappears: this time she is wearing a jewelled belt, the ends of which cross and hang down on the left side. The jewels are not like any known to us, being large and of fiery luminosity, and the belt is made of something that shimmers like golden chain-mail of extremely fine texture.

18

The Mermaid of Sandside Head

It is interesting to compare Geoffrey Hodson's preceding account of mermaids (or undines) to the observations of seemingly ordinary and non-clairvoyant individuals. While some tales of mermaids from ancient times may be mere fable, or the sightings of seals, it is not so easy to scoff at stories which are more recent, and which do not have the "feel" about them as having merely been made-up. For example, in 1809 a learned society of Glasgow heard that a **Mr. William Munro** *of Caithness had witnessed a mermaid, and most of them expressed total disbelief. To try to get to the facts, one Dr. Torrance wrote to Munro, who was a schoolmaster. Perceiving that Torrance himself appeared open-minded, Munro wrote in reply, in a letter which was published in* The Times *on the 8th September 1809.*

This mermaid of William Munro's was apparently seen by many others beside himself. These sightings lasted for an hour or more, and could be made at times from within a distance of just twenty yards. If these stories are all true it is a most unusual case, not least because the mermaid was visible to so many, and did not flee or vanish.Munro wrote:

About twelve years ago when I was Parochial Schoolmaster at Reay, in the course of my walking on the shore of Sandside Bay, being a fine warm day in summer, I was induced to extend my walk towards Sandside Head, when my attention was arrested by the appearance of a figure resembling an unclothed human female, sitting upon a rock extending into the sea, and apparently in the action of combing its hair, which flowed around its shoulders, and of a light brown colour. The resemblance which the figure bore to its prototype in all its visible parts was so striking, that hand not the rock on which it was sitting been dangerous for bathing, I would have been constrained to have regarded it as really an human form, and to an eye unaccustomed to the situation, it must have undoubtedly appeared as such. The head was covered with hair of the colour above mentioned and shaded on the crown, the forehead round, the face plump, the cheeks ruddy, the eyes blue, the mouth and lips of a natural form, resembling those of a man; the teeth I could not discover, as the mouth was shut; the breasts and abdomen, the arms and fingers of the size of a full-grown body of the human species, the fingers, from the action in which the hands were employed, did not appear to be webbed, but as to this I am not positive. It remained on the rock three or four minutes after I observed it, and was exercised during that period in combing its hair, which was long and thick, and of which it appeared proud, and then dropped into the sea, which was level with the abdomen, from whence it did not reappear to me. I had a distinct view of its features, being at no great distance on an eminence above the rock on which it was sitting, and the sun brightly shining.

Immediately before its getting into its natural element it seemed to have observed me, as the eyes were directed towards the eminence on which I stood. It may be necessary to remark, that previous to that period I beheld this object, I had heard it frequently reported by several persons, and some of them persons of whose veracity I never heard disputed, that they had seen such a phenomenon as I have described, though then, like many others, I was not disposed to credit their testimony on this subject. I can say of a truth, that it was only by seeing the phenomenon, I was perfectly convinced of its existence.

If the above narrative can in any degree be subservient towards establishing the existence of a phenomenon hitherto almost incredible to naturalists, or to remove the scepticism of others, who are ready to dispute everything which they cannot fully comprehend, you are most welcome to it from,

Dear Sir,

Your most obliged, and most humble servant,

WILLIAM MUNRO

19

'What I Saw Was Real'

Another mermaid was seen, nearer our own time, in 1900, by **Alexander Gunn**, *a highly respected small landholder of the Scottish Highlands who died in 1944. He told his story in Gaelic to a collector of tales and legends of the Highlands. If the story is not true, it is difficult to see the motive in telling it. Gunn made nothing from telling of what he saw, and can only have lost local credibility. Moreover, his experience took place in north-west Sunderland, in the district of Sandwood, which also happens to be known as "The land of the mermaids". And when the account was published in 1948, the author, R. Macdonald Robertson, to whom Gunn had told the tale, also noted that more recently two girls walking on the shore of a sea-loch in the same area declared that they had seen a mermaid slip gracefully off a rock into the water. Their description was similar to that of Gunn's. Alexander Gunn's own encounter is summarised as follows.*

He had gone down a gully leading to the sea with his dog - to rescue a sheep which had got wedged in the gully - when his dog uttered a howl of terror. He looked up to see a mermaid reclining on a ledge only six or seven feet away. She was very beautiful, and of human size, with reddish-yellow curly hair, greenish-blue eyes and arched eyebrows. Her back was also arched, and the look she gave him was both frightened and angry. Mr. Gunn was frightened too, and ran off (we are not told whether the dog had already abandoned him, or whether he was abandoning the dog!), realising that she had been stranded and was waiting for the next tide to float her into the sea. But, he said in Gaelic to Mr. Robertson: "What I saw was *real*. I actually encountered a mermaid."

To myself at least, this story has the touch of authenticity. Which leaves one mystery still remaining. Clairvoyants describe various categories of undines, including the typical mermaid, as being another kind of fairy, but of a different level of matter-energy to earth fairies. Yet all the accounts from non-clairvoyants such as Gunn's, that of William Munro, and many others I have details of, which seem to be spontaneous sightings made by ordinary individuals, describe apparently quite solid creatures which "slip" into the water or are "stranded" waiting for the tide. There are also eighteenth-century accounts of mermaids supposedly being "hit" by oars, out of fear, or even stoned to death. To this mystery of how the non-physical undine of the clairvoyant might relate to this other apparently fully-materialised version of the mermaid I confess I have no answer to offer.

20

Findhorn's First Contact

The most well-known example in the twentieth century of human beings consciously co-operating with nature spirits is that of the Findhorn Community in northern Scotland. People from all over the world have lived or attended courses there, and have come away with a greater appreciation for the need to recognise the reality of the nature spirits behind the outer manifestation of nature, and to work with them. The Community is still most famed for that which first brought it to international attention: the growing of miraculously large vegetables, of flowers which bloomed wonderfully out of season, and all this achieved in the often biting cold of that part of the world, and in a "soil" which was little more than sand. The plants have not been "miraculous" since the 1960s - except insofar as any plant is always a miracle. It is as though they simply appeared for a time as a sign and a signal to bring in the thousands of people who have contacted Findhorn, that their souls might also be more nourished in the sands of this world and in its sometimes cold life.

But what of that beginning? In a sense, Findhorn began when among just six people living in a caravan, the intuitive spiritual contacts of Dorothy Maclean were combined with the practicality and inquisitiveness of Peter Caddy. The rest being history. It was 1963, and as Dorothy MacLean later recounted the first times:

Our first winter at Findhorn had been an especially harsh one for the area, with frequent gale-force winds adding to the snow and rain. But by early May, 1963, the first radishes and lettuce Peter had sown in the patio garden were coming up, and he was busy preparing another area for peas and beans and a few other vegetables. The spring weather was growing warm enough for us to sit outside on the patio during our daily time of quiet together. This was a delightful opportunity to experience God's presence in everything around me.

During that period of time, my guidance had been telling me to be open for new ideas and inspiration: *Be prepared, My child, and on the lookout for My promptings. Expect new ideas to come into your head. This is a further period of training for you and it entails many things.* The guidance I received on the morning of May 8 was indeed the beginning of something new: *One of the jobs for you as My free child is to feel into the nature forces, such as the wind. Feel its essence and purpose for Me, and be positive and harmonise with that essence. It will not be as difficult as you immediately imagine because the beings of these forces will be glad to feel a friendly power. All forces are to be felt into, even the sun, the moon, the sea, the trees, the very grass. All are part of My life. All is one life. Play your part in making life one again, with My help.*

Well, I thought that was very nice, because as far as I was concerned, there was nothing I would like better than to sit in the sun and commune with nature. But when Peter saw this guidance, that's not how he understood it. "You can use that to help with the garden!" he said, feeling that direct contact with the nature forces might give him the answers he needed to his questions about the garden.

Sure enough, the next day I was told in guidance, *Yes, you are to cooperate in the garden. Begin this by thinking about the nature spirits, the higher overlighting nature spirits, and tune into them. That will be so unusual as to draw their interest here. They will be overjoyed to find some members of the human race eager for their help. That is the first step.*

By the higher nature spirits, I mean those such as the spirits of clouds, of rain, and of vegetables. The smaller individual nature spirits are under their jurisdiction. In the new world these realms will be quite open to humans - or I should say, humans will be open to them. Seek into the glorious realms of nature with sympathy and understanding, knowing that these beings are of the Light, willing to help, but suspicious of humans and on the look-out for the false, the snags. Keep with Me and they will find none, and you will all build towards the new.

I thought such instructions rather a tall order, taxing my credulity and certainly beyond my talents. I knew only a little about nature spirits and, although I was aware of the angelic hierarchy, I had not known that there were devas overlighting vegetables. I told Peter I couldn't do it and stalled for several weeks, despite his encouragement. However, instructions from the inner divinity - and Peter's promptings - are not lightly disregarded!

One evening in meditation I reached a powerful state of heightened consciousness, and I thought, now I'll contact one of those higher nature spirits. Since vegetables had been mentioned, I thought I might contact the spirit of some plant we were growing at Findhorn. I had always been fond of the garden pea which we had grown at home in Canada, and I could feel in sympathy in all ways with that plant. So I tried to focus on the essence of what the pea was to me and the love I felt for it. I got an immediate response in thought and feeling which I put into the following words: *I can speak to you, human. I am entirely directed by my work which is set out and moulded and which I merely bring to fruition, yet you have come straight to my awareness. My work is clear before me - to bring the force fields into manifestation regardless of obstacles, and there are many in this man-infested world. While the vegetable kingdom holds no grudge against those it feeds, man takes what he can as a matter of course, giving no thanks. This makes us strangely hostile.*

What I would tell you is that as we forge ahead, never deviating from our course for one moment's thought, feeling or action, so could you. Humans generally seem not to know where they are going or why. If they did, what a powerhouse they would be. If they were on the straight course of what is to be done, we could cooperate with them! I have put across my meaning and bid you farewell.

When I showed this to Peter, he said, "Fine, now you can find out what to do about these tomatoes and what it is these lettuces might need. And I would take his questions to the deva of the species concerned and get straightforward practical advice.

21

Cottage-Sharing With Leprechauns

Tanis Helliwell, *a Canadian of Irish blood, has been able to see elemental beings since childhood. While still a young girl she "erected a screen" to stop her clairvoyant and psychic abilities entering her consciousness, in order to be like and "accepted by other people", who had demonstrated fear of her. Then in her early twenties she opened herself up to other realities again. Years later still, in the 1980s, she went alone on a spiritual retreat to Achill Island of County Mayo, Ireland, renting a cottage there for the summer. Here she finally re-established the conscious communication with nature spirits which she had abandoned as a child. Her extraordinary summer began upon first entering the cottage...*

After a half-hour walk, I came to a small, white cottage with a slate roof and a blue door surrounded by a white fence. The cottage matched Mr. Davidson's description, so I opened the gate and walked up to the door. I was surprised to see that it was ajar and called out, "Hello, anyone home?" No one answered, so I tiptoed in.

There was a fire blazing in the hearth. I let the pack drop to the floor and sat down on the nearest chair. As my eyes grew accustomed to the darkening room, I slowly took in my surroundings. There was a pile of peat beside the hearth and a bellows standing nose-down beside it. In front of the hearth was a saggy old green couch and, behind that, a large wooden table with six very sturdy chairs. To my left was a small empty room, obviously not used, and to my right was a door through which I could see a window and wardrobe, suggesting a bedroom. Behind me was a tiny kitchen which served double duty as an entrance way.

Since entering, I had felt as if I was intruding on someone's home, as if someone had left for a few minutes but would soon return to discover me. I tried to push this feeling aside, but more and more I was convinced that I was being watched. More accustomed to the fading light, my eyes swung over to the corner from which these vibrations emanated. I was shocked to find four people watching me: a small man, a small woman, and two children. I froze in place, not breathing. I've walked into someone's home, I thought, but what strange clothes they're wearing. My God, they're not human! Within milliseconds I concluded that I was in a haunted cottage, with mounting hysteria.

Before I could proceed along this line of thinking, the little man addressed me.

"We've lived in this cottage for a hundred of your years and we're willing to share it with you, but we have some conditions."

His appearance belied the authority of his words. He was no more than four feet tall and was dressed in an old-fashioned, buttoned-up green jacket that ended at his waist. It fit tightly over a fully rounded tummy. Brown trousers, cut off at the knee, extended down to thick leggings, which were inserted into large clog shoes - larger, by all standards, than his feet had the right to be. And completing this strange attire was a gigantic black top hat.

The two boys were miniature versions of their father, minus the protruding stomach and top hat. They were fidgeting,

obviously trying to behave but wanting to be somewhere else doing something different.

The little woman was dressed in a full skirt down to the floor, underneath from which peeked the same style clogs of her husband. She had on a hat that reminded me of those worn by the New England pilgrims, which seemed too large for her head. Her red hair was drawn back in a bun, but pieces refused to be confined and were busy falling down even as I looked. She was having a hard time keeping her hands still and kept wringing them, then putting them behind her back; next she'd smile at me and then, looking at her husband, she'd remove the smile and attempt to look serious.

The little man composed his face into a look of forced patience while he waited for me to respond to his offer. I was thrown off balance. Still, I had the feeling that some unexpected opportunity was awaiting me - something unlooked for but precious. I responded, matching his serious tone.

"What are the conditions?"

"We're willing to strike a deal," he countered, seemingly relieved that I could speak.

"What's the deal?" I asked defensively. I was beginning to suspect that the "we" was really an "I," and that the little woman and children were there merely as backup.

"Well ... you're living in a haunted lane - and not all the elementals here are friendly to humans."

"Excuse me," I said, wanting to make absolutely sure that we were talking in the same language, "but what do you mean by 'elementals'?"

"You humans," he said impatiently, "call us gnomes, goblins, dwarfs, faeries, elves, and leprechauns, but we're all elementals. Now, as I was saying, we'll protect you for the summer. I know you'll need this protection because I know why you're here."

I almost stopped him again when I heard that, but decided I'd find out in due time. He seemed to realize my attention had wavered, because he paused before continuing.

"In return, at the end of the summer," he said, "I'll ask you for a gift."

"What's the gift?"

"We'll not tell you now. We'll tell you at the end of the summer," he responded.

Somewhere in my foggy memory bank I recalled stories of humans being tricked by faeries and elves, and I was leery of striking any open-ended deal. I could say that I didn't have any choice, as this was his cottage and I had nowhere else to go, but that wouldn't have been quite true. I believe that I could have lived there physically for the summer and simply closed myself down to these little people so that I never saw them again. But what unimaginable experiences would I be shutting out at the same time? And deep down I had a feeling that he would make a fair request. It was almost as if, even then, I was trusting him, so I said, "I agree."

22

The Fairies of Venus Hill

Marko Pogacnik *of Slovenia (of the former Yugoslavia) spent many years practising the healing of areas of the earth, including by his method of "lithopuncture", which is literally the acupuncture of the earth with special stones. Arising no doubt from this life-long attunement with the earth and its energies, on January 26 1993 Pogacnik found himself in communication with the realm of elemental beings for the first time. Over the next thirteen months, under the direction of various of these nature spirits, he completed a book describing in detail his experiences working with the intelligence in nature. He focused in particular on what he perceived and was instructed had gone wrong between the respective kingdoms of humanity and of the elementals, on how man's actions had created havoc in the nature kingdom, and how to heal the rift and work in harmony with the beings of the elements. The following extract, from his annual summer's retreat on the island of Srakane, is noteworthy in its reminder to us that to simply* see *nature spirits is only to perceive the tip of the iceberg of what they are actually involved in doing and are a part of. Here, Pogacnik details four levels at which the fairies of place he saw on Srakane were all simultaneously active.*

To strengthen the credibility of... messages from the myths, I would like to tell the story of a host of fairies which I watched in summer 1993. I was on the Isle of Srakane, a small, stony island which is part of a group in the Adriatic

Sea (the group includes the other tiny islands of Susak and Srakane Male).

I perceived that the focus or 'umbilical cord' of the fairies was a tall, thin pillar of power on top of the central hill, which I named Venus Hill because of its inner connection to the Planet Venus. The pillar of power was anchored inside the earth and was glistening with all the colours of the rainbow as if it were woven from delicate coloured threads. In my consciousness I immersed myself in the pillar of colour to be carried upwards by the ascending power.

At one point, about a hundred metres high, the pillar of power resolved into a group of dynamic beings. I identified them as fairies of place for this location. They expanded from their centre in a gliding motion until they covered the entire area above the group of islands. As soon as they reached the borders of their territory they would return in a big sweep to their source at the focal point. In this resting phase they resembled the closed bud of a flower. After a pause, these white fairy figures would expand outwards again and glide through space on the same route. It resembled the movement of a constantly opening and closing flower bud.

I tried to count the number of individual beings within the host of fairies, and got a surprise: there were 13 of them. To be honest, I must confess that I had been quite certain that, in accordance with the normal rules of invisible reality, the number would be the solar 12, and I felt a certain resistance when it turned out to be 13. When I asked within for a reason for my resistance I was led downwards in the pillar of light. Deeper and deeper I followed the fairies' focus, through the crust of the earth and into the underworld. There I saw the thirteenth fairy circling like a shadow through the underworld spaces. At first I believed that I was seeing a demon, and I was afraid. But I soon realised that the work area of fairies of place could not be restricted to the air *above* ground. To be complete, their sphere definitely had to encompass part of the dark world below.

I immediately remembered the dark, thirteenth fairy in *Sleeping Beauty*. She was not invited to the birth celebration of the newborn princess, but nevertheless appeared to tell the princess that she would die at the age of 15. This thirteenth fairy reminds us of the moon rhythm[1] and the old world order. Within her own being she was not negative at all; rather she represented a darker part of our world sphere together with the underworld aspect of the fairies which had been banished from our consciousness at a time when memories were still fresh of these fairies of place in their light bodies.

I asked myself what it does to the life of a landscape when fairies of place dance in concentric circles, since this kind of fairy dance is often mentioned in fairy tales. In response I recognized four levels on which the fairies of place were active. On the uppermost level the fairies would show themselves in harmony with the rhythm of the stars and planets. These rhythms were reflected in the fairies' consciousness and would put them into a state of ecstasy. They would transfer this state of being to their surroundings and at the same time would imprint the cosmic time pulse onto all living beings.

The next level below this one I can only compare with the feelings of ecstatic love-making. This derives from the fairies' constant gliding through their area, and the scent of unconditional love which they wrap around even the tiniest

---

1 The ancient lunar calendar with 13 months was replaced by the sun calendar with 12 months.

living particle with which they come into contact. The whole area is repeatedly bathed in the love of these divine beings.

On the next level, the fairies take care of all the different life processes which occur within 'their' space. It also entails the alignment of the earthly life rhythm with the universal rhythm, as well as the orchestration of various patterns of events within the nature kingdom to guarantee the most harmonious life atmosphere.

Then I was able to see the fourth level which connects their work to the underground spaces. Here there is a feeling of grounding and deep rootedness within the being of Planet Earth.

Finally, I must stress that we should not imagine the four levels of fairy consciousness as being four hierarchical layers; rather they are expressed in each moment as four interweaving vibratory qualities, and they are danced by the fairies.

Since we humans hold more and more power over our shared living landscape, the fairies of place are no longer able to limit their function to the nature kingdom alone. During the past centuries, without being conscious of it, human culture has striven to shape and occupy spaces, and has had an impact on the fairies of place. The relationship between the two formative forces will become increasingly tragic because we human beings are completely ignorant of the function of these fairies. We force our egotistical will onto the landscape without consulting the lawful intelligence of the fairies about the effects of our interventions. This is true even of some of the well-intended ecological projects of which we are so proud.

23

'Don't Sit! There's a Fairy on the Chair!'

Philosopher-architect and mystic **Peter Dawkins** *was born in Edgbaston, Birmingham, in 1945. Gifted with an intuitive sensitivity and clairvoyance from a young age, during his childhood he developed a deep love and awareness of nature and the angelic world, and a growing sense of the energies inherent in the environment. He studied architecture at St. Catherine's College, Cambridge, graduating in 1967 with a BA (Hons) which was followed by a Diploma in Architecture and an MA. Whilst living and working in Scotland in the early 1970s Peter experienced a series of visions of a revelatory nature, leading him directly to a specialised knowledge of landscape temples and their energies, and to the work he now does with people and the environment. In 1974 Sir George Trevelyan encouraged Peter to give lectures, lead pilgrimages, and share his growing knowledge more publicly. Since then he has given many hundreds of seminars, lectures, workshops and Summer schools in the UK, Ireland, Germany, Denmark, Holland, Belgium, France, Switzerland, Spain and the USA. He has also led over fifty major expeditions and pilgrimages world-wide, and written several books.*

Since 1978 Peter has given up architectural work to devote himself to Landscape Temple Science and also Baconian-Rosicrucian work. In 1980 he founded the educational charity, the Francis Bacon Research Trust, and in 1988 began to develop a training course for what he then called the Temple Science. In 1994 he gave the name Zoence (the Greek word Zoe means 'life') to his teachings; it is a synthesis of all his studies, researches, discoveries and experiences over the years. I happened to briefly meet Peter in 1997, and it was soon obvious to me that he enjoyed an intimate contact with elementals and devas. Even then the idea entered the back of my mind that it would be fascinating to interview him, and when this book was nearing completion I arranged to do just that.

David: *I deliberately didn't find out much about what you're doing in respect of elementals before this interview, in order to keep it fresh.*

Peter: Yes, well we do a lot of workshops now to introduce people to the concept of elementals, and to try to help them to feel them and see them. So it's become quite an important part of our work. I have a Zoence course which includes a specific workshop on the nature beings, and that leads on to angels and so on. So it's part of the training we do for Zoence. And then we do a special week on Iona. We are also going to Ireland in spring to look at fairies and so forth.

But the Celts used to call the whole lot fairies, right up to the great gods. So it can be difficult to know where to draw the boundary with angels or devas.

There is a need for a New Age taxonomy for such beings, perhaps.

Yes, there is a definite hierarchy, and we are trying to work out a common language. Different people having different experiences are using different words to grade the hierarchy. Then they hear of other people's terms, and slowly there is a common language appearing. For example, the word 'deva' is Sanscrit, and literally means 'shining one'. But at Findhorn it was used to refer to landscape angels, so I have taken that on board and use it in the same way. I work a lot with landscape angels, and these are the angels that appear at sacred sites. For example, you might have a mountain angel which could be a landscape angel, and it is throwing out a whole pattern of energy which makes a complete chakra system on the landscape. It's astounding. We work with big and small ones, but there is always an angel behind it, an intelligence behind it. I see them as the thought-forms of the universe. And that thought-form or intelligence produces these energy patterns that nature then forms itself in accordance with.

Then within that there can be smaller angels responsible for certain parts of that landscape, and then I would use the Findhorn term, deva. But the terminology between different people can be muddled. And the same coming back to fairies. Fairies seem to be what people call the beings which work more with plant life, as distinct to those working in the earth, the dwarfs and gnomes and so on. I have found there is a definite set of nature spirits that really do concentrate on working with plants. They work within certain areas, and over them is a deva, over that whole area, and they are like the workers for that deva. They work with the plant life, and they take energy to and fro between the plants. Sometimes I will see them with a face, and they will stay stationary and project what they want to project. So I think they a project a form, whatever they want to us, so we can recognise them.

At other times when they don't stop and are busy doing work, I see them as spinning tops of energy, and they are very, very fast, and they dart from plant to plant. They may want to go round and round the plant, sometimes up and down it, and they'll go on to another one. And they can be beautiful, absolutely beautiful. Some can be very small, and some of these beings, though I'd still call them fairies, looking after plants, are actually quite big. Some that I've seen were two or three times the size of a human being. And it's wonderful, they are lovely.

When was your first experience of seeing fairies, or have you seen them all your life?

It was when I was 28. I can't remember seeing fairies at all as a child, but for as long as I can remember I've seen angels. But I've not seen nature beings, until I was 28. I moved to Edinburgh, following my fiancée who was at university there, and we got married there. After we got married, we went to a mid-summer festival at a Steiner school. We were invited to go. We sat with the parents and watched the children dancing around the fire. And there was an orchestra. It was all outside in the garden.

As they were dancing, I saw movement in the bushes. I looked, and then I saw these circles of fairies dancing. It was extraordinary. I didn't expect it, it just came into my awareness. And then I saw there was another circle nearer the dancers, not hiding in the bushes, and they were trying to copy the children, and they were having great fun. They were falling over each other and laughing. They were just fantastic, and they were enjoying the whole festival. That's my first experience.

And then Sarah, sitting next to me, had to go to the loo. And while she was away one of these fairy beings came up to me and stood in front of me. In size, with me sitting down, he came up to just above my knees. He had his hands on his hips, and he had a pointed hat. But actually the hat was a flame. His whole face, his whole head, came up to a point. But it's possible to interpret it in the classic terms of a dwarf. He introduced himself to me, he said his name, and then he started talking to me. He talked about lots of things, extraordinary. And then he hopped up and sat on the seat and seemed to be sitting next to me. I say 'seemed' because

78

it's not physical, but it was very real. I've learned that every physical thing has its etheric counterpart, so he was really sitting on the etheric chair.

Then my wife, Sarah, came back, and she was about to sit down. But I yelled out, "Don't sit! There's a fairy on the chair!" And she leapt up as though it was on fire! It was so funny, I'll never forget that. And then of course the fairy moved, and she sat down. She wouldn't have hurt him anyway if she had sat down, but he was so real that I felt that she would squash him.

Then after that, I think it was the very next day, some friends wrote to me for help. Because they live in the south-east of England, and in their whole area, a large area of land in Hampshire, the ground was falling away into holes. A whole hospital nearly disappeared. The holes were very, very deep, and nobody knew what was going on. It was a mystery, and everybody was very worried. It was on quite a big scale. And they asked me if I would tune in. So anyway I tuned in to this gnome, because he was really a gnome. He came to me again, and he actually introduced me to his family of gnomes, and how they worked with the rocks and stones and crystals. His family actually worked with quartz crystals, to help bring them to perfection. So I went, in my meditative state, into his realm of consciousness, where crystals were like water, waterfalls. The gnomes bathe in them. Everything is very different, but very real.

And then he addressed the problem I had been asked to look into. He took me down to meet (this is in thought), the nature beings in the landscape of the south-east, and I was shown the problem, which was to do with water and its use. The water table was going down too quickly, and the underground rivers had changed their course, causing a collapse from above. In fact the fairy life was very angry.

Actually, a few weeks later the scientists were brought in to see what was wrong, and they came up with the same answer. That's exactly what it was. The water table had gone wrong. So it was funny that out of all the fairies he was the one who came up to me, and immediately I had this problem to look at. It was almost as if he knew, and it was all set up to get me involved. Then after that my contact with fairies was very good. I see them intimately, I see them all the time. But I have to tune in, it's a question of attunement to get them. But sometimes I can be in the right state of mind, and not trying to look at them, but spontaneously they appear right there.

So for people who can't tune in, what is the best way for them to work with fairies, if they want to but they can't see them or talk to them?

Well, if they want to, that's the first thing. If you want to see the fairies then you've got to believe in them. You've really got to. Otherwise, non-belief absolutely blocks the line, blocks consciousness. Presuming that someone wants to see them, and believes in them - which is not always the case, because some very sceptical people who don't believe in fairies say, "Well, I want to see them for proof," but that doesn't enable them to see them. So it takes someone who is open-minded to make friends with them. I think that people can't see the fairies but they're in that state of mind where they can feel them, their presence. Actually I think it is possible for everyone to see them ultimately, but you have to start with the feeling, and then you train your mind to see them.

This is a very big question, but if elementals were able to say something to the people of the world right now, what do you think it is they would say?

I think they'd actually say, "Come on, get on with it. Do what you are meant to be doing, which is being gardeners of the world." We are born to be gardeners of the earth, and the gardener looks after the place, and helps every plant to grow to its best possible being - tree, vegetable or flower. That is what we are meant to do, and that is what fairy life does. Of course, they cannot very easily move physical stuff, but they can move etheric.

We do a lot of pilgrimages, and in pilgrimage we work with energy to help it flow, just like on the meridians of the body. If you go into certain places it is like acupressure, you can create a whole movement of energy on the meridian. And if you walk along the meridian it is even more powerful. But pilgrimages are basically going from place to place. You take the energy with you as you go. And I suddenly realised - actually, in Slovenia - I was followed by these nature beings, and I suddenly realised they were pilgrims. That's what they do with each plant, the fairies. They are pilgrims, taking energy from plant to plant. So they are all linked to this energy which feeds the plants with life. To me that was quite a revelation.

Among the four kingdoms of elementals, salamanders are thought by some people to be the highest or most spiritual elemental. Have you ever had any experience with salamanders?

Yes, and they're like fire, they're mischievous. Or they can be mischievous; they can be your best helper. It depends how you approach them, but even if you approach them well, it's like fire, you have to be careful. Really the elementals are the spirits of their elements. So they have the intelligence which gives their element its qualities. We've gradually learned to work with them, and if one's serious, I find it's no good to keep asking them to do things all the time, but if there's something important, then it's possible to ask them to help, if they want to. I don't want to ask them against their will (laughter).

How do salamanders appear to you?

In the flame they are a kind of dancing form. They don't live very long. It's not just a trick of the imagination. They do a certain work, and they can talk and communicate. But they don't seem to have long lives, unlike fairies. The same with sylphs of the air. Whereas salamanders literally have a fiery nature: they appear, look at you, and then they're gone. But the sylphs, literally their movement is like that (demonstrates) through the air. Sometimes it's very slow and graceful, and sometimes they go faster.

Then the undines of the water - they also have flown, but it's very different - and their nature seems to be very happy and joyful. They are very playful. And then you get the elemental beings of the earth. But I don't see the gnome as being an elemental. The gnome is something more than that. So, to me, there needs to be another name. But again, it's the consciousness of these elementals which is the deep and fundamental thing. It's different to ours at such a fundamental level it is difficult to put into human man terminology.

So do you think it is best for people who don't actually see these things to tune into nature as a whole?

Yes. It's not good to try to force the ability to see elementals. That's not the way it happens. Those who try to force it may then simply be seeing their own creations.

Have you experienced the relationship that elementals have with music, and how they associate with music?

Yes, music exerts a very direct effect on all the elementals and fairy elementals. The best example I have seen of a good effect was in Ireland. I was taking a pilgrimage there, and there was one lady who was so fey, she was so attuned to nature and to nature beings, but she wouldn't say that she could see them, but she could feel them. And she was a master player of the penny whistle. It's very difficult to play the penny whistle, and she could play like a magician. On the pilgrimage, every now and again, she would suddenly go away from the group, and she would go and stand or sit down, and play. And blow me, if she hadn't chosen every time a place where I could see masses of these fairy beings and elementals. They used to come pouring out just to listen to her music. Some would dance, and some would just sway, and it pulled them all together. And when she finished she would know when to finish, she was so in tune with them. And they would go out reinvigorated, I could see them shining.

So to me that what was one of the best examples I had ever seen of how music helps them. Stunning. She knew she was playing for them. Each time she said, "I was called. They called me. I must go and play for them." She played from the heart. She played Irish folk tunes too, but usually it was all created spontaneously. And very often, another thing that was interesting is that I could sometimes see these places were particularly full of fairies; I was thinking of pointing it out to the rest. But she would be off to that spot before anything had been said. But I know from another instance she was not just picking it up off you, she was attuned, which was great. The Irish are very good at this (laughter).

It has been such a big experience, ever since I was 28, and I'm 52 now. So it is a continuing experience with me. Especially in either Ireland or Iona I get the biggest experiences.

Well, that's a question, actually. Many people live in big cities today. Do you think the likelihood is very much less of there being elementals in such places?

Well, I think it's certainly easier for human beings to tune in, in the right consciousness, in the countryside, and to experience them. But then again, some people say, "Oh, you never get them in cities. They don't like city life." But it's not true. They are everywhere. And if they were not everywhere I think nature would die. But where nature is dying there are not many elementals or fairies around. So to me they are very much connected. Elementals are the life-forces of all living things. And if we do the wrong things it causes these life-forces to retreat.

I have also seen another way that elementals are repelled. I've seen it is possible through people's thoughts for them to build bubbles around themselves. In that bubble is their thought atmosphere. And these bubbles can expand right to where the fairy beings live, and the fairies can get pushed away by the wrong sort of consciousness. That's been very real to us.

So in the big city you are unlikely to find nature spirits?

Not in some places. But in other places people love plants and nature, and that then draws the nature beings there. So there you have the reverse happening. You get someone imprisoned in a house or flat, and all they've got is a terrace or a balcony. But they are so in love with their plants, even inside the home, and that draws many fairies. Because they don't just walk on the ground, they can be up in the air and come to the tenth storey of a block of flats.

In fact I had a wonderful experience when I was in Germany, with Peter Caddy funnily enough. They kept inviting me to do workshops there, to go into what fairy beings I could see, and Peter wanted to compare it with the Findhorn experience. One day I was out in the garden with a group, and a gnome came up and really wanted to talk. Well, I was trying to say something else to the people, but he went, "No, no! Talk to me." So I took the whole group there, and he talked a bit, and then he said: "These trees are dying." He was quite categorical about it. "They are dying. They need a certain mineral," he said, "and you've got that mineral in the house." And it was all Double Dutch to me. So I repeated this to Peter, and he said, "Oh, yes, I have." He went to the house and he had a whole pack of a certain type of ground rock with these minerals in, which he'd been given some time before and had never used. We used this on the ground, and it revived all the plants that were dying. That was a great feeling, a great thing to happen.

And then another time I was in the garden, and I was with the angels. We did a whole ceremony, a fire ceremony. There were a lot of people there, and it was really quite wonderful. Then these new angels came, and one appeared to me overhead. It opened up like a big aeroplane opening up its doors, and out poured masses and masses of nature spirits. They just poured out of this angel and came down to the garden to add to the atmosphere, so the number of nature spirits there were increased. But they came from the angel. And I have had other instances where the nature beings are like cells of the body of the angel, each cell having its own work to do. Very interesting.

It seems that there are many books out about angels now, and people are much more aware of angels. Now it seems it's time for nature spirits to also have their day.

Yes, isn't it ... (then to a friend:) The balloons! (laughter) This shouldn't go in the book, really. Well, yes, we can tell it.

Most years we go to Iona in September, just after the equinox, for a week's retreat. We go with about 40 people, and take over a hotel. The subject is usually on either angels or the nature beings, because that island is so wonderful for that subject. This occasion was on nature beings. And they wanted a party! So by the time we had been there a few days we realised a way to give thanks to the elementals was to give them a party at the end of the week. This is very serious (laughter), and funny, but that's what they asked for. So we arranged this for the last day, Friday. And so we are going to have a party. We got party things and we blew up balloons. And the locals had this view of 40 people hiking it from the hotel to the southern part of the island with boots on, and anoraks, and rucksacks with picnics in, and hats on against the weather - which is very mixed on Iona - and balloons going up from the back packs! And chocolate, everything like that. It was so funny.

There are two parts to Iona, the northern part and the southern apart. And in between there is a kind of low lying part that leads to the area of Machair, which means "common ground", on the western side facing the Atlantic. It's a big, wide bay. You have to get there on your way to the southern part of the island. So we got there, and we were closing the gates. But the balloons kept popping, for no apparent reason. We were getting a bit worried about it - would we have any balloons left? Then we got to the start of the southern part of the island, which is real fairy territory, it's like their kingdom.

We've learned to find energy gateways, and stop and tune in, and ask permission to go in. So we stopped at this place, and it also happened to be 12 o'clock. So being mid-day, we had a prayer for the world, stopped in front of this energy gateway. Then it's time to move off, and I was just about to lead the others off, and in front of me were these two fairy beings. They were like guardians of the gateway. And somebody asked the question, not knowing they were there, not knowing I was seeing these beings, "Why do our balloons keep popping?" And immediately these two fairy beings said, "Oh, we thought balloons *were* for popping!"

It was so funny. I've missed the point of the story too. Just before that, people had been debating, "What's the purpose of the balloons popping?" You know, "Perhaps it's all our holy breath going out into the world to heal it," you see. All these great high falutin' ideas. And the fairies just simply said, "Oh, we thought balloons were for popping!" - which was such a deep and funny wisdom, balloons also being your inflated egos and minds, and so on. There were lots of levels to it. And they do tend to teach like that. They have this great sense of humour, but behind it there's a real wisdom.

24

Humanity: You Must Manifest a Different Face of Creation

Mark L. Prophet *(1918-1973) enjoyed an intimate communion with elemental life. Though he spoke of his contact with elementals, most of what he said, told to the people around him during the course of his life, is now either lost through forgetfulness or due to the passing on of those who heard him. But he did sometimes speak about the elementals in public, and this was tape-recorded at the time, for posterity. More recently it has been transcribed, and some of this forms the present chapter (see Bibliography and Reference Notes).*

Born an only child in Chippewa Falls, Wisconsin, his father passed away when he was nine, and he and his mother had then to endure the hardships of the Depression years. As a boy of eighteen, while labouring on the Soo Line Railroad, he was contacted by the Mahatma El Morya. El Morya is one of the same Masters who were the sponsors of Helena P. Blavatsky, and who were behind the founding of The Theosophical Society. But Mark Prophet had been raised a devout Christian, and at that time he rejected the tall, powerful, turbaned figure who appeared to him in a mystical experience. Later he told of how, having seen the light, he spent years praying for El Morya to come to him again.

Morya did so, and from 1952 to 1958 Prophet was Morya's amenuensis or messenger, taking down the Master's dictated letters or "Ashram Notes" to copy and mail. In 1958, under the direction of the Master, he founded The Summit Lighthouse organisation for the spreading of the teachings of El Morya and other Ascended Masters. The Summit Lighthouse exists to this day under the spiritual direction of his wife, Elizabeth Clare Prophet.

There are numerous tales those who knew Mark Prophet can recount of his attunement with the beings of nature. Should important building work be underway as winter would normally set in, Prophet seemed able to hold inclement weather at abeyance until the work was complete. There were times when rain would either stop or start in obedience to his mighty call. Once he was observed on a motorbike being followed by a miniature rainstorm that only surrounded him: when asked about this extraordinary phenomenon he simply replied that he had been "playing with the elementals". This is his testimony on the subject of elemental life.

Many years ago there lived an author, Gene Stratton-Porter. Some of you may have read her *The Keeper of the Bees*, and various other works such as *Girl of the Limberlost*, and so forth. This young lady seemed to have a peculiar attunement with the elemental side of life and an awareness of God, an awareness of man whereby she conveyed very beautiful spiritual concepts in her novels. Apparently, she belonged to the higher spheres of consciousness and did not live to be very old but passed on to the higher realms of light, leaving behind the legacy of these very beautiful and wholesome novels.

I think that many of our dear friends of the Light have taken great interest in gardening through the years. And I know that many students of the Ascended Masters do have a tremendous love for nature. So I think it would be well if we would turn our thoughts now to review some of the rather unknown side of nature.

Like everything else that is visible, the flowers and the fruit trees and the growing things are produced, not by happenstance or chance, but by cosmic law. And the elementals are the divine intelligences that are charged with the maintaining of the form and texture of the flowers, the leaves, the stalks, the plants, and everything that is produced.

Now, I used to have the idea and I had it for many years, that God created everything and then from that point on, that the things just took over and continued as they were, it's like a clock with perpetual motion. God wound up the clock and set its works into position and the clock just kept going tick-tock forever. I was quite amazed then, when the Masters began to reveal to me this wonderfully interesting side of life concerning the elementals. For as a boy when I would read the fairy tales that are usually taught in school I was of the impression that they were fairy tales.

Well, they were, but I just didn't believe in fairies and I thought it rather strange that the Irish people should actually discuss the little people as though they really existed. And I said to myself, "Is this not a very strange thing, that so many intelligent Irish people, really intelligent people, actually speak of fairies as though they existed?"

Then I read of different cases where they had been sighted in the glens of Ireland, and I decided that the only people that had fairies in their back yard were the Irish. But I found out afterward that people in other parts of the world also seem to know something about elementals and fairies.

When Walt Disney came out with his production of *Snow White and The Seven Dwarfs*, again I thought it was purely a cartoon and a creation of the mind of Walt Disney based on fairy tales and so forth. Though I was impressed with the musical score. You remember that one, "Hi ho, hi ho, now back to work we go," you know?

Well, I found something happening inside of me one day. I have a built-in projector. It works through the light of my heart. And it projects pictures that come from the higher octaves on the screen of my mind. This is not a joke or a tale, no matter how I'm telling you, it is truth. And I'm sometimes shown pictures of past civilizations and the internal workings of people and their consciousness, as well as that of animals and other things. There are a variety of subjects. I'll find the light in my heart, it comes focused through a film that comes from higher octaves and actually projects a picture on my mind. And I see back into time and I see truth revealed in a series of pictures.

Now, I am not gullible, to tell you the truth, at all. I'm difficult to convince of anything. I do not have the conceit of knowing that I know all things. I feel that God knows all things. But I have tested this, these concepts, and when they meet with divine approval and I get the feeling from the Holy Spirit of the great truth in them, then I know that the picture is correct.

I do not, nor have I to my knowledge, had any revelations ever given to me that were not true in this regard. I don't, in other words, have a series of pictures where a hundred of them come through and ninety-seven of them are good and accurate and three or four are bad. As a rule they are all good, and they're clear. So I want to pass on to you some of the knowledge that I have obtained by this method concerning the elementals.

Elementals as God's Arrows of Consciousness

I have become aware that every single manifestation in nature is presided over by elementals. That there are no flowers growing anywhere, even a blade of grass that is not presided over. So there must be an awful lot of elementals when you consider this. Now isn't that true? And this is something that I have come to realize - that there are many, many, many elementals. There has to be.

Actually, in one sense you can think of an elemental, strictly speaking now in the mechanical manner, as though God had a quiver of arrows of thought and he pulled all these arrows out of his quiver, he pulled them all out at once, he put them all into this one bow, and then shot them to earth. Not as in the poem, "I shot an arrow into the air, it fell to Earth I know not where," but with direction. All these arrows of his consciousness go up. Every elemental is like an arrow, it has a target, a mark that it wants to hit. It's a concept. In a sense the elemental is a puppet under God-control. Well, this is true also after a limited fashion.

And I think basically one of the reasons why people do not know as much about the elementals as they do about other parts of creation is because we do not know as much about God as we think we do, perhaps. Because the elementals are very closely linked with God, even though they have a lesser stature than the angels.

Probably most of you are familiar with the passage of scripture that says that man was made a little lower than the angels yet crowned with more glory. Well, the elementals are a little farther down the ladder. They are, in one sense, also our brothers as the angels are, but we think less about elementals because they range all the way from probably a little shorter than the nail on my little finger to as tall as some of the great redwood trees, the giant redwoods.

Naturally, elementals are usually not visible to mortal sight, although on rare occasions they have become so. I think it's rather sad, perhaps, but the world takes little notice of what they cannot physically or objectively see. The world takes great notice of what they can see and that's why they say, "Clothes don't make the man, but they make him look better." We all look better if we wear something that looks well on us.

Now if you lived on a farm in Texas and you went out your front door and got in your car and you started down the long road for the ranch gate, and you had a big enough ranch, you might get so far away that you couldn't even see your house, even on a flat spot. You know what I mean? You could get so far away that when you'd look back, it would look just like a nub sticking out of the ground, and a few other nubs here and there, and you wouldn't recognize it at all. Well, the house would not be invisible, would it? Would it be invisible?

It's out of range. And this is exactly what we have to contend with when we stop to think about elementals. They are not really, actually invisible. They're out of the range of ordinary human sight. And, therefore, you can see elementals if you know how to refocus your consciousness and your eyes and other faculties that you have that are spiritual in nature. This is one of the things Adam and Eve lost, you see. We were supposed to be able to see and commune with elementals, and talk to them just as we talk to one another. And that lost art of communication between angels and man, and between elementals and man, is the cause - that's the missing link causing the whole cosmic plan to go awry and be aborted.

People can't even see them (but they can see people). And therefore they're ignored. People say, "It's a fairy tale!" If anything is more horrible, it is that, that the enemy - and you have to realize this is a deliberate plot and plan, no more diabolical plot or plan has ever existed than to make these elementals into fairies, and then people laugh about fairies and they say, "Oh, it's only fairy tale." Well, this is why truth is stranger than fiction. Because there is nothing truer than the manifestations of the elementals. Some outlive us by many years, I mean. Elementals can live a thousand or two thousand years. They die, but they do live a long time. And there are some pretty old elementals with long grey beards. They even grey.

They are very much a part of God. Now, we have to realize that the Godhead is very much divided and subdivided and yet completely unified. This sounds a little bit strange at first, but it's not so strange at all if you stop and realize that Almighty God himself, if it required it, is probably not going to come down here and paint a little flower. He probably would not paint your gladiolas. This is a pretty big job painting a gladiola. It's a little too small for the great Lord himself to do, but it's a very important thing for us. And the same is true of a carrot. We wouldn't be here in the physical octave if our bodies were not sustained.

I realize that many are aware of the value of certain health foods. You probably participate in a good healthy diet whenever you can. Well, if there were no vegetables or fruits upon the planet, where would we be? Some people have the idea that these things are like Topsy, "they just growed", they were created and that God put all of the qualities in the sea for the continuation and expression of nature and that nature just goes on automatically. And that's all.

Well, it isn't because we know that if you go away on a trip, on a vacation, and you have a beautiful front lawn, many types of grass will just keep growing like your hair and when you get back, you're going to be out there manicuring the grass. Why? Because it's probably two or three inches higher than when you left.

So you see all nature, if it's going to be modified and refined, requires attention. And the kingdom of heaven, the kingdom of God, the kingdom of nature is no exception. So the function of the elementals is the sustaining intelligence behind every manifestation. In other words, if you have a bluebell or a buttercup or a forget-me-not or any kind of flower, there is a pattern for that specific flower or fruit which originally came forth from the mind of God. This is a blueprint, it's a divine idea, and this divine idea is given to an elemental.

For example, if you want a forget-me-not, the pattern for the forget-me-not flower is given to an elemental and that elemental sustains in consciousness the image of the forget-me-not and oversees the creation of that flower for each season. There are billions and quadrillions and infinite numbers, almost - I realize that it's not truly infinite on earth. But the number is beyond our imagination. And the service of the elementals is tremendous.

So the elementals are real, and they are tangible, and they have thought, and they have feeling. Now here's what I'm trying to show you in this thing. This great stream of energy that comes from the throne of God, of life and of consciousness, comes through the consciousness, first of all of the mighty beings known as Elohim. And from the Elohim it is stepped down to the level of the Archangels - to Archangel Michael and the other Archangels. Then it goes down from there to the Chohans or Lords of the Rays, who as many of you know are advanced Ascended Masters, ascended from the human kingdom. And it's dispensed through the Maha Chohan, or Great Lord, who is also the Maha Chohan of the elementals. Then there are four kings over the four kingdoms of elementals. Because every elemental belongs to one of the four elemental kingdoms of fire, air, water or earth. The first king of all the elements is Prince Oromasis who is the prince of the fiery element. And Prince Oromasis is in charge of all the salamanders, the beings of the flame that have to do with transmutation. Prince Oromasis has a consort, a divine consort, the feminine aspect of himself, who is known as Diana. So Oromasis and Diana are in charge of all the elementals of fire.

Then you have the air. And who do you think is in charge of the air? Aries and Thor. Aries is actually the masculine being here, and Thor is the feminine part, although you'd think it would be the opposite way around. But in this case the term, Aries, is the balance. And so Aries is in charge of all the sylphs of the air in the whole world here. That's the king. You've heard in the Norse mythology of Thor's hammer. And this, of course, is the clap of thunder which is supposed to be Thor's hammer. But there is something behind it all.

The king of the water is Neptune, and the counterpart of Neptune is Luara. And so these two control the water element. All the undines are under them.

Now we come to the gnomes, and the gnomes are all under the protection and direction of Virgo, the Earth Father and Pelleur, the Earth Mother - Virgo and Pelleur.

I wanted to paint the picture - necessarily simplified - of how the energy and divine direction of God himself descends through the different levels of hierarchy. So you see, all four elements have their elemental kings, and each have millions and billions of elemental beings or nature spirits under them. And these beings are in charge of the production of blades of grass, of minerals within the earth, of the air, the turbulence, the flow of the tides, all the things that take place in earth, air, fire and water.

The Gnomes and Their Activities

Part of the work and function of the gnomes of the earth is to work with the precious minerals. And *Snow White and the Seven Dwarfs* did a beautiful job of presenting that earth elemental to mankind, of bringing them to mankind's awareness. They're short of stature, they're puckish, impish, not exactly too attractive at times, and they actually create and wear clothing that is very odd in shape. Like stocking caps pulled over their head with little bells on, and things of that kind. They actually design these things themselves, and they dress very oddly.

They sometimes play leap-frog together. A whole group of them will come out of a cave and one will bend over and the rest will all leap over and they'll just go leaping right along the ground. They do a great deal of work you see, down in the lower parts of the earth. They can walk right into the ground.

Now, first thing you're liable to tell me is, "How can they do that, because I can't walk in the ground?" Well, if you were made up of a hundred tennis balls, and we put you into a pail and we threw you at a fence that had holes in of a certain size, you'd go through, wouldn't you? We know matter is not truly solid. Well, gnomes interpenetrate earth just as easily as we live in air. You have any trouble walking around in the air? You don't, do you? The elementals can walk right into the ground, and they do. They go to underground streams and rivers.

Of course they do feel the density of the earth when they pass through it. This they have told me. They feel the solidity of the earth, and they find that it is not as easy for them to walk through the earth as it is to walk on the earth. Consequently, they only walk through the earth when it's necessary. They prefer to use the subterranean passages that exist from one continent to another under the ground.

And they walk sometimes in great armies of them down there.

One time, a whole army of elementals left China and Russia and came over to the United States because of certain conditions that were imposed upon them over there. They became very unhappy concerning some of the conditions of the Chinese people and the Russian people. And as a result the wheat harvest went way down, a tremendous drop in the wheat harvest.

We had a dictation concerning it. And a fiat was made by the great being, Kuan Yin, to the effect that because of the Chinese actions in keeping children living in communes that the forces of nature were going to rebel. Almost immediately after that dictation the wheat harvest dropped and dropped. Then, of course, the tremendous amount of wheat we had stored in America became a pawn in the world game of politics. And ultimately we did sell some of that wheat to Russia as you may remember from reading the papers.

But coming back to the elementals, you have to understand that the whole cycle of life is manifested through them. They are responsible for the growing of the food. Without them, food will not grow, you'll have famine. And you know, the elementals get involved in karma. When India has so many famines, you have to understand some of the reasons for that famine. There are certain things that the Indians do that ignore the elementals. They ignore them. They give so much devotion, actually, to various what the Christians would call pagan idols. They have the wonderful cult of the Mother, of course, and they have all their different worships of God in his different aspects and different names of the Hindu pantheon of deities. But they very seldom pay any proper attention to the elementals. Therefore every once in a while they are swept by a famine because there is not enough gratitude given that reaches the elemental side of life.

The gnomes of the earth, now. In fact, the deposits of gold, and all the mineral deposits of the world, are actually created by God, through the gnomes, as seed deposits. The energy of the sun goes through the earth and forms a magnetism. And gold and silver deposits grow in the earth. But they grow under supervision - just as vegetables do in a garden, and this, of course, is something that science doesn't know and doesn't realize. But it is absolutely true. They grow in the earth, and the gold is more or less taken from the sun. It is the energy of the sun, a certain activity of the sun, that creates gold.

The gold is very precious to the earth because it holds a spiritual balance, and it does have great spiritual as well as financial value. That is why the gold standard is very important, and why a nation should have a lot of gold deposited in its country. And of course, that's why the enemy wants to get all the gold out of America. Because that will take away the great power from America if they can get away all these gold deposits, the bullion we have stored at Fort Knox and other places. The same applies to other nations too. So these elementals, bless their little hearts, do a wonderful work for mankind by creating and tending these deposits and seeing that they expand.

Now of course, what actually happens is, that these deposits don't grow so rapidly that you could see it in one lifetime. Mineral deposits are much slower in their processing. Another example is the whole carboniferous cycle where of course diamonds are created from coal. This is part of the crystal ray, we call it, that makes up the diamond, the crystal ray from the throne of God. That is why diamond has all that iridescence to it. Yet it starts from a simple lump of coal, which shows the process of refinement and transmutation. Now that's the earth elementals at work.

The Undines and The Jellyfish

But we have another type of elemental that is extremely important to us and that is the water elemental, the undine. There is a ballet called *Undine.* You may be familiar with it. This is the realm of the meermaid, or mermaid, connected with the sea. The water elementals, of course, control all the fish and mineral life in the sea and the water element all over the world.

You are interacting with the energy of undines even when you use water for washing your body, or for drinking purposes. And your body, by the way, is composed of a tremendous amount of water. About eighty percent water. And there's twenty percent something else. Well, we're almost like a jellyfish aren't we? We have an awful lot of water we're carrying around. A lot of it is in the blood of course, and lymphs, and digestive juices and enzymes and other things. This comes from the water element. So we really owe a lot to the water element as well as the earth element.

And our vegetables are composed of both water and minerals, are they not? And vitamins, of course. Which is a fancy name for life. Vita-min, life for men. Women too!

Sylphs, and the Causes of Storm

Now then, we have another type of elemental and that is the air elemental or the sylph. You better make friends to these elementals. They're beautiful. These are the type of fairies you see with the long golden hair and the rather thin, seraphic type bodies, and they're very curvaceous. They float through the air and they'll bend their whole body in different shapes. Sometimes the body is bent with the legs behind, trailing like a garment and their arms in the most graceful ballerina poses you can imagine.

They have beautiful faces like the most beautiful women you can imagine, except that they're faces of purity. I mean there's nothing hard, or there's nothing carnal in their faces. They have a very beautiful face. The only exceptions are of course that certain sylphs take on the more human form. That is, they take on human attitudes when they are subjected to them.

Now the sylphs, when they do take on negative human attitudes and qualities and human discord, will desire to rid themselves of it, so they do it with centrifugal force. And in order to rid themselves, or to throw off this human vibration of hate and anger, they start a whirling action in the air. And they don't get dizzy either! They can whirl so fast they can develop winds of a hundred and twenty or even a hundred and fifty miles an hour. There's no stronger force known to man that the force generated by these air elementals. That's the power behind the hurricane. These sylphs are tremendous forces, dynamos of whirling energy. And they dissipate their energy in destructiveness back upon mankind.

I thought it was rather interesting that in a *Pearl of Wisdom* sometime back, our weekly published dictations from the Ascended Masters, we were told that there was a tremendous focus of witchcraft in the state of Louisiana, one of the worst in the country. And we found that this hurricane made its way to Louisiana. Rather interesting if you stop and ponder the subject. So you see, you have a plastic nature in these sylphs, they will take on and mirror human attitudes and bring about destructiveness.

For the elementals have two sides to them: they're do-all, dual. They have their divine mission to carry out. But the elementals do have a consciousness of their own which is something like the negative of a film. When they are exposed to light or to energy, they tend to pick up the radiation of that energy and to express that energy along with the divine pattern that they were given charge of, do you see. And they are great mimics, and of course, that's how thorns came into existence. Thorns came into existence because human beings had sharp thoughts. And people tended to work around the bushes and the elementals outpictured these sharp thoughts.

Now nature changes, Luther Burbank found that out. You can govern the change and direct it by grafting together two types of trees. But the elementals have to merge or the life force won't stay in there and the tree would die. So Luther Burbank found out that he had to love these elementals, and he worked with them through love. He sent out love to the two elementals, the lemon tree elementals and the orange tree elementals. And of course, the result was the grapefruit.

Well, many of you like grapefruit as I do, I'm sure. It doesn't have the tartness of the lemon exactly, and it doesn't have the sweetness of the orange, but it is a very delicious flavour. I especially like the pink grapefruit, I imagine that's because it has an awful lot of divine love in it. A very juicy, delicious fruit. But we see that the elementals will mirror our actions.

Marc Anthony, he said, "Friends, Romans, countrymen, lend me your ears. I came not to praise Caesar but to bury him." He started out by getting them on his side, and he wound up having inflamed the mob until they were ready to put an end to the life of every single person that had wronged Caesar. He accomplished what he wanted to by the subtlety of agreeing with them first, and then turning around afterward and bending them to his will.

So you see, this is what happened, actually, as far as the elementals were concerned. The elementals are very easily influenced. They're more easily influenced than a child. For example, wrong thought and feeling poured out in a small town day after day by husbands and wives fighting, could result in a tornado hitting that town. That's right! A tornado can be generated if none was ever intended, by the thoughts and feelings of the people in that town, if the elementals pick it up.

The sylphs can be controlled and they will work for God's children. They respond to prayers and dynamic decrees. I remember driving an automobile near the city of Chicago, Illinois. And as we arrived in the vicinity of Chicago, the entire area was black with storm clouds. It was an absolute scene of terror, because in those storm clouds were cyclones and tornadoes.

So when we perceived the ominous and threatening danger to the city, our entire group in the car immediately went into action contacting the sylphs of the air. Prior to our first beginning, the storms and the winds began to howl. They howled something terrible and they sobbed as a child would sob. We all heard that sobbing. But amid the wind we made our decrees, we sang to the elementals, we called for the dissolving of the storm, and it was all done exactly as we called for. The whole storm clouds disappeared and the city was saved from terrible destruction by the calls to the elementals.

And this is the secret method that Jesus used to still the waves when he spoke the fiat, "Peace, be still!" When he sent out the vibration of peace to all the elementals, the waves had to obey, because the elementals were only making a fuss because they were disturbed. When he gave them peace, they were no longer disturbed, and therefore the sea ceased its raging.

The elementals are reflections of man's thoughts and feelings. And the displays we see in nature of storms, of lightning, of thunder, of cataclysmic action, the sinking of continents, all of this, or the rising even of the continents, whatever - all of this is a manifestation of man's consciousness reflected in elemental life.

You will find this in the statement, "In sorrow shalt thou bring forth thy children and thou shalt eat thy bread in sorrow." And then it says, that "the forms of the earth shall appear." And, "you shall till the ground," you see. "Cursed be the ground for thy sake." This is a statement that God made involving the elementals. "Cursed be the ground for thy sake." And man's inharmony transfers to the elemental side of life the curses of the laws of karma, and actually brings discord into the elemental kingdom, which ought not to be, of course. But it is man who does it, by disobedience. It is man's karma. And it is by obedience and by love that we are able to help the elementals.

These overseers - the elementals, they are overseers - were created by God to function at all times and to carry out his action in a correct way. In the original days of the creation of the Earth, for example, we did not have the condition known as rain. Nature functioned in a more heavenly way.

Now, the elementals are very sensitive and they pick up what is called the matrices of God or the matrices of man almost on an equal basis. Man was originally created in the image of God, so just see happens when man starts to become inharmonious. Let people start becoming very angry with each other and of course the elementals pick this up. Cataclysmic action is based on human greed, human anger, human distress and human outpicturing of the works of Satan rather than the works of God. The elementals pick this up, the elementals manifest it.

The elementals are plastic, then, in consciousness to a great degree. The pure thoughts of God at hand in nature are always divinely functional. But man has been given dominion over the earth. He has been imbued with God's energy and has been given free will. And in many cases he has misused that free will in misusing the life-energy of God.

The mind may influence the elementals, but the emotions influence the elementals a great deal more. When you are distressed and downtrodden in your heart, if you feel wounded, storm clouds may suddenly appear in the sky all over the city, especially during wartime. Many people are familiar with the episode of Good Friday when Christ was crucified. There is a song written by Wagner called the *Good Friday Spell*. This illustrates how the Good Friday spell or pall was cast over everywhere by the darkening sun because the Christ was being crucified, and all nature rebelled against it.

Whenever you see activities of wrongdoing occurring in the world, as a rule the reflection of that will be in nature, and the sylphs will react and storm clouds will be produced. Because they reflect the distresses inherent within man.

The Story of Milarepa: The Karma of Misusing Elementals

Now then, you also have the fiery salamanders. The great master, Milarepa, is quite an authority on salamanders. His story is not very appetizing, and is about the wrong employment of fiery salamanders, which are fire elementals, for the purposes of black magic.

Milarepa was a young man and he was about to get an inheritance, and he had an uncle and aunt who were defrauding him and his mother of this inheritance. And he was unable by legal means to thwart this uncle or prevent this act of infamy, so he went to a black magician and apprenticed himself to him in order to learn how to destroy his uncle.

He was taught how to go into a round tower and invoke the fire elementals. He had to hang up certain symbols on certain spots on the wall, and he invoked this fire elemental and forced it into the form of a giant scorpion. One of his cousins was enjoying a wedding feast, but by black magic Milarepa filled the house with vermin, and then materialized the giant scorpion. It was the size of a yak, and Milarepa had it pull down the central pillar of this house. Thirty-five people died in that collapse, but Milarepa allowed his aunt and uncle to live, just so he could torment them further, which he did. He would conjure great storms of hail, rain and fierce wind to destroy their crops. So this was actually the misuse of his power to force into evil acts the elementals of water and of air too.

Well, the time came when at the age of thirty-eight he spiritually woke up. Then he was horrified when he saw what he had unleashed, like in the *Sorcerer's Apprentice*. He got a bitter taste in his mouth and I think if he could have brought those people back to life and put everything back the way it had been he would gladly have done so.

You know, vengeance is not something that after you get it, it is as sweet as people might think it is when they try to seek it. Because those one seeks vengeance against are a part of God, and all parts of life are part of God. How can one part of God be at war with another part of God? You see. That's why there's no right for vengeance, but there is a right for defence of truth and right. That's a different action now. But human vengeance, the desire to wreak havoc upon someone that may have wronged you, or you think may have wronged you, this is dangerous, as Milarepa found out. He was sick to his stomach and he was horrified in every manner.

So he went away from the house and the abode of the Dugfa. The Dugfa is the black magician. And he left there and he journeyed to the home of Marpa, a white magician. Marpa saw him coming, and he could smell his aura probably miles away, and he couldn't stand Milarepa. He said, "Get out, I don't want you near me." Milarepa said, "My Lord, I've come to be your chela." Marpa replies, "I don't want you, leave, go, get out."

Milarepa knew enough about the law that he knew the Master had to receive him if he threw himself at his feet and placed himself at his mercy. So he did. The guru didn't like this at all. He was fuming! I suppose he was being tested too, and he tried his best to discourage Milarepa. He did everything but swear at him, and he was a holy man too. This was a terrible trial to him, because Milarepa had the stench of death and abomination, in his very aura. But he said, "Very well, I'll receive you."

And for years and years he put Milarepa through the most terrible tortures. He says, "Before you can find God you've got to build a house. And it's got to be built of stone. You've got to build it while stripped to the waist out in the hot sun." And Milarepa did. And he got a sunburn. The sunburn was cruel and it broke into blisters. He was very unhappy and he sweated and he toiled. He got the house half up, the guru came along and he looked at it and he said, "What are you doing?" Milarepa said, "I'm building a house as you told me to, my Lord."

Marpa took his foot and he pushed all the boulders down one after the other until they all tumbled down. He said, "Start all over, it's not good." He did this again and again, until Milarepa was almost beside himself. He even beat Milarepa. Marpa knew what he was doing though, and this was all to break Milarepa's human self-will so that he could live instead for an ideal. And finally after years of this and other tortures the guru took him in and he said, "Now, we'll start you in on the white magic disciplines, teaching you how to do the right thing."

So he gave him tremendous tests, and finally and ultimately Milarepa was put into a cave where he had to sit cross-legged and meditate twenty-four hours a day. He had to sleep in this position. And he ate very little food. Eventually, he became so emaciated and hungry that he reached up to where there were green nettles growing in the wall of the cave, and he reached up, he became so hungry, and he plucked these nettles and he ate the nettles till his body turned green. He took the colour of the nettles on, had a pale green colour to his body, and he was just practically nothing but skin and bones.

Some came by in Tibet there and as they walked past and looked in the cave, they saw him there and they said, "Oh, buta." Not "Oh, Buddha" now, but buta, a ghost. They thought Milarepa was a ghost, a buta. So one says, "No, I don't think it's a buta, I think it's a yogi in meditation." So they gave him a little food.

And then, after a time his sister came. She got some mutton broth together. He was walled up in the cave, you see. He had a wall and a little hole about a foot probably in diameter. And she reached through and he took the bowl with trembling hands and then he ate this mutton broth and was strengthened. He went on living in there for years until finally he expiated his karma.

All of this torture lasting for years and years and years for having followed the left-handed or black path. His torture was so terrible that it isn't even all recorded, what he went through. But he really paid for it, and the reason he did so is because he determined that in that embodiment he would right all the wrong he had done and not spread it out over many embodiments. So he did.

He became a Master. And he learned to fly, and levitate. The women in the fields of Tibet would be out harvesting the grain and they'd see Milarepa flying through the air overhead and they'd say, "There goes that crazy yogi, Milarepa, again." He was flying long before aeroplanes.

So ultimately he became a great Master and his fame spread throughout the land. But then the people, they became very jealous of him. And they decided to kill him. So some wise men and jealous men of the local area - Sanhedrin, I'd say - I mean these were the local boys engaged in the practice of religion. They finally visited him and they arranged for the poisoning of his food. Well, he knew it was poisoned when he ate it and he didn't try to stop the action of it, but he ate it. He had enough mastery for the poison not to touch him, but he said his time was come anyway. He was in his eighties. So he died and they burned his body. Though even that wasn't before he resurrected it again right there in front of them and sang a hymn!

At his cremation suddenly flowers began to fall through the air. Roses fell, and the perfume of the roses could be smelled all over the streets. At that cremation a huge mandala appeared, right over the area, filling the whole sky. Because it was proof that he had been accepted by heaven itself, and the wrong and inequity that he had done was now corrected. Everywhere in Tibet today it is recognized very definitely that Milarepa became a master and a true follower of God.

But you see how terribly foolish it was for him to dabble with black magic? I want to adjure one and all, don't ever dabble with black magic, Satanism or anything like that. Keep your consciousness pure and loving toward God. Because the pathway to God is not really difficult.

The elementals under Oromasis are the most difficult and dangerous elemental forces in existence anywhere, because fire is a raging force. When it is correctly used, it can assist you greatly. But when it is employed by black magicians, as happens all over the world, it is the most destructive action under the sun.

Salamanders: Dragons, Or Your Best Friends?

These are the beings of the flame. The fiery salamanders are the most powerful of all the elementals. The fiery salamanders are the ones the black magicians employ when they really wish to do a terrible, evil work, because the fire elementals are the highest form of elemental life.

The fire elemental, when misqualified by black magicians, can be so horrible that it is actually the horror that is behind some of these horror movies that the powers of darkness bring forth through Hollywood. They create horror in movies purposely in order to lock a certain thing into people's consciousness that is evil. They lock images of horror into people's consciousness and into their subconscious. And God is not that way. There exists no horror in God at all. This is all human. It is all a manifestation of the black magicians. So it's wise to cut down on watching T.V., and to be cautious of what your eyes look upon. But they use the fire elementals to do this, and they affect the emotions of mankind by the fire they have imprisoned into wrong matrices, wrong forms, wrong activities. They get one salamander, one fiery elemental, and they can do tremendous activity with it. But when an imprisoned fire elemental breaks loose, watch out.

Elementals ordinarily are not dangerous. And I have many friends among the fire elementals. And Oromasis is the most magnificent, magnificent being. I remember when he first spoke through me in New York City, I thought I was a candle! And I thought my clothes were actually going to catch fire. I'm not joking. It was the hottest hot that I have ever felt!

So fire elementals are real and they are employed by black magicians, and also some white magicians too, but frankly, I am more concerned that all men and women become cosmic adepts and attain union with God. I believe what we should strive for is to follow the Christ in the regeneration. This is, after all, the very meaning and God-intended purpose of life. So many, many people are caught up in the idea of black magic and in the manipulation of others.

The story of Milarepa, of course, shows us that sin and the stain of sin - in other words, negative karma - can be wiped out. But it also points out the severity of the punishment for the employment of God's holy energies in the wrong way. And I think some of the most sinned-against elementals have been the fire elementals. Because they are the biggest and hugest elementals of all. They were used to ensoul the bodies of the dinosaurs and dragons in the early days when black magicians first created the animals. The misuse of energy actually goes back that far, even though it is said man wasn't around then. And this is where the legends originate of the fire of the dragons, you see, with the fire coming out of their mouth. Because the fire elementals were put into the dragons, and this was a terrible action. These fire elementals are huge.

You know how fire can be. It can sweep through a forest and be very tall. The biggest gorillas could be ensouled by fire elementals. And the black magicians on Atlantis used these fire elementals for making war against each other. This is a sinful thing, because the fire elemental, when he's correctly understood, is a very beautiful being and is very close to the heart of God. This is the highest elemental. It's the spiritual elemental actually. Because the universal life-force and the sacred fire are all closely connected. And the fire elemental is so plastic, so completely free from the grosser elements of matter.

You see, the fire elemental can destroy all other material. Fire can consume all of the earth. Fire can even burn the oxygen in the air. Fire can even burn water. It can take the oxygen out of it and can convert it into steam and then even just vaporise the steam. So fire is the most powerful of the four elements.

The right use of fire, the right use of water, the right use of energy always brings happy homes and happy hearts. But believe you me dear people, the world is just going right on using energy wrongly.

In other words, there is a certain thing I want to state: "If the righteous scarcely be saved," St. Peter says, "where shall the ungodly and the sinner appear?" So we really probably will only slide by, and we're lucky if we can get by into the ascension, the true goal of life, by a thread. So why should we turn around and waste our energy in fruitless activities that will only involve the soul in the snare and the pit of negative karma? We have to pay for everything we do. Everything we do that's wrong, we have to pay for. Everything we do that's right we are rewarded for.

And what a wonderful thing the law is. How constant and beautiful the law is in its constancy. Isn't the law wonderful? Supposing the law was practising the concept of the favourite son, which concept a lot of people have, that God favours one person and disfavours another. In actuality the favour of God is captured by what we do and what we think and what our motivation is. If our motivation is pure, then we're all right. Because we're going to work out our salvation with fear and trembling if our motivation is pure. That's the important thing: the motivation. Why do we want to do it. If we want to do it to please God, he knows that, doesn't he?

Now, Walt Disney, I'm sure on the inner if not on the outer, was well aware of the elementals. And in his *Fantasia*, he actually showed the victory of life through the whole life cycle, where man, angels, and elementals come into union. In the closing scene of the film where the music changes from the *Night on Bald Mountain* from Mussorgsky, to *Ave Maria*, it is the shift from the mood of the elementals in their dark cycle to their light cycle when the change occurs away from the vibration of human thoughts and feelings of horror, of fear, of anger, of witchcraft, of the invocation of evil, and all these conditions that are negative, and of darkness.

And what happens when you replace it? You hear the church bells ringing, you begin to sense a feeling of the eternity of life, and you see the parade so great that you can't even see the end of it, of people coming up the mountain. No longer is it *A Night On Bald Mountain*, no longer is it an absence of good, a presence of fear and terror, but now the sunlight is coming up, the dawn over the hill, everything is joyous, and you hear the *Ave Maria* ringing out in the church bells. Your whole soul feels relieved that all this is over.

So I'm trying to show that the world of visibility that we have is nothing compared to the invisible world that is all around us. And the elemental beings are affected by man. This is what has caused earthquakes in divers places. The elementals are so affected by people's thought and feeling. But also other people are too.

Embodied Elementals

Now here is something rather interesting. We know of a few elementals that have made the grade to leap from the elemental kingdom into marriage with men and women on this planet. So we have a few people on this planet who are part elemental and part human. I've seen them. I'm sure you've seen them too on the street, but you didn't realize it.

Now don't ask me exactly how it is brought about. It may be that they are able, under God's law and with his blessing, through some method to impregnate mortals with life. I don't mean physically, you understand, but to spiritually enter into the human birth process. Thus the father or the mother would be a fully material earthly creature, and the offspring of this strange relationship would be half mortal and half elemental. So it does occasionally happen. It is the means for the elementals to bridge the way into immortality. They can never possess immortality under the present scheme of cosmic law except through marriage to an earthly being which gives them a threefold flame activity within their heart, and enables them to step up in the hierarchy of cosmic evolution. So a little elemental can actually unite with the human being and they can have a child. But this is an inner action, it's not something outer. So don't try to conceive of it as a part of the orderly birth process.

This is the one way that an elemental can become immortal, to pass through the human kingdom. There is, for example, the case of the Ascended Master Fun Wey who was originally an elemental. And he was put upon the knee of the Ascended Master Eriel, he and another elemental. And Fun Wey became an Ascended Master through the human kingdom. He was first an elemental, and then he was granted passage into the human kingdom, and eventually he ascended and is today an Ascended Master.

But there's another trek that can be made. Some elementals bridge through to the human kingdom, and then they take a jump into the angelic kingdom. Going through the angelic hierarchy, they may finally even become an archangel, and this has happened.

What I like about this is the fact that it illustrates the principle of rise. It illustrates that God has embedded in nature a man's opportunity and a woman's opportunity to be exactly what they really aspire to. If you want something, you can have it, you see. Isn't that really great? If you stop and think about it, it gives everybody a chance. You don't have to be satisfied with your present attainment or circumstances in any way, not with any part of yourself. Because God has provided the process whereby you can transcend it all. Because God has not fixed the appointing of the bounds of man's habitation. He has not fixed any limitations of spiritual attainment to humans, elementals, or to angels. He does not stop us if we really want it badly, you know.

Of course you can't just say to yourself, "I'm going to become Archangel Michael," and then become Archangel Michael! But you yourself could in some other solar system or universe become an archangel, if there is room for an archangel. In other words, if it isn't all filled up. There generally is room but sometimes you have to move to another galaxy. Unless others graduate on further and their offices and roles need filling. There is an expansion process going on through the whole universe, however. God just keeps creating. It's fantastic. It's truly fantasia.

Moreover, talking of Archangel Michael, it just so happens that he once *was* an elemental, a tiny elemental. He has told us so. So in a way he did 'decide' to become Archangel Michael. But he didn't just say it, and it happened! No, it took millions of years of effort and of embracing God's will to progress so far.

When elementals cross into the human kingdom, naturally there is a tendency to take on and embody the qualities they bring with them. For example, in Switzerland there are several elementals that I know of, people that are embodied there that have a certain very stocky build with ruddy cheeks and so forth, and this is because they really were gnomes before.

I think there is a possibility that some dwarfs are actually elementals in the early process of transfer. Later on, as a rule, there's an elongation of the body, and as they are re-embodied, perhaps two or three times, they may heighten up a bit and look more like an ordinary person.

Then you have elementals that have crossed into the human level who have the characteristics of the sylph. And these are usually very thin people. The ladies are very thin and very well poised. They have marvellous control of the body and they make excellent ballerinas.

Then, of course, you have water elementals, who are very emotional people sometimes, and usually quite fat because they take on a lot of water in the body. Their whole glandular system will be oriented to drawing a lot of water into them. If these people become angry they often will have less control, because of the fact that they are too much orie-nted to the water side.

Fire elementals are usually very brilliant. They have a memory capacity that is almost beyond belief. And these people are often very outstanding-looking people. They look so exceptionally different to other people, the fire elementals when they embody. But they are always half human, remember that. They never come in pure; they are half-human.

Elementals in Grief, in Dance, in Music

So it shows that it is possible for elementals to rise out of their little niche and become a great deal more than that. I'm telling this because I wish to develop a certain picture here and make it clear that the elementals play an important part in the scheme of things, but because the mortal - as opposed to the God-ordained and immortal - creation of form is transitory and passes from the screen of life, they themselves are transitory, and they have a limited span of existence.

Now, it was not until human greed began to manifest upon the planet and mortality replaced immortal, God-centred existence, and people began to die, and with their death express grief at death, that the elementals, observing the human grief-death cycle, also started to grieve when their own passed on. And they had a great deal more cause for grief because although some of them had lived for a thousand years or more, they are not immortal. Therefore when their father dies - for they marry and have children just like we do here - when their father dies, then their father is dead. When their mother dies, she's dead. There is no return or re-embodiment for them. They go back to the Great Central Sun for repolorization. This means that their substance and energy returns, but not the individuality. They simply reach an end to their cycle and new elementals that are born are taking their place and the process goes on.

I've seen an elemental funeral. One was laying there and they all gathered around and they hung their little heads with utter dejection. The pathos of it was so dreadful that it was far worse than a human funeral because human beings have some hope of immortality. The elementals know that when they go, they go.

Now in a dictation he gave through me, beloved Jesus gave a fiat that has taken the sting of death from elemental life. At our Easter conclave of 1964 he endowed nature with the momentum of his resurrection flame. He said that this dispensation would:

> make it possible for them to feel, throughout their manifestation as an elemental, a part of the radiance of immortality which I AM. Do you see what this means? It means that they shall no longer be aware of death.

Do you know what this means! Contemplate, contemplate, contemplate nature, conceived by God and designed in the higher octaves, lowered through the elementals into manifestation, now endowed with the flame of my momentum of the resurrection this day that forever after from this day forward the elementals shall never again have the sense of death!

Though they pass, it shall be as the click of a camera shutter or the dropping of a bird on wing when its beating heart stops - suddenly they shall be here and then they shall be gone, but without pain or quiver of fear.

They shall feel my flame always. A portion of that flame resting in them shall remove for all time immemorial all that fear that they have outpictured.

And this is one of the first steps as we begin the process of quickening the world for the golden age, enrobing it in the garments of eternal spring. For the eternal spring must first come into the invisible world and the world of the formless and then be outpictured in the world of form. And the love of the students for the elementals and the decrees and the fiats and the prayers, both of heaven and earth together, have made this possible this day .

This is a manifestation of the greatest hope, and it is one of the first steps in the abolishment of all death everywhere.

All over the planet today, because of that fiat the elementals have a greater feeling of joy because they are not now in stark awareness of this coming event that casts its long shadow before them. So they execute in a more charming manner and happiness all of their functions upon the planet.

Well, the elementals were always happy, as you probably realize. And actually, the little elementals are the ones who have given to mankind the gift of the great and beautiful steps of the ballerinas and of the ballet. The ballet steps so beautifully executed by some of the great ballerinas and ballet dancers in Moscow and New York, and all over the world, originated in the elemental kingdom.

Almost all the ballerina movements that are used by mankind today are borrowed from the movements of the "little people." You know, the swift executions of pirouettes, how they turn around and how they'll leap into the air. You've watched both men and women do this in the movies and on the legitimate stage. These movements, which are executed under duress by mankind because they take years of training, are quite natural to the elementals. And the little gnomes and fairies can leap for joy, and they do. They have their circles in the grass, and they dance and frolic with great delight.

You can go into some of the sylvan glens in Ireland, as well as in the United States and elsewhere, and with spiritual vision you can see some of these elementals dance. You may see this elemental who may be no higher than two or three inches. He will dance and pirouette around, and then he'll suddenly leap into the air like the ballerinas do, and he'll go up and cling to the very edge of a little branch right over, say, a rose. And then he may fasten his legs on, and hang upside-down. He'll hang down directly and reach down into it and sniff the essence of the rose, just like people will smell of the flower. Then he'll suddenly twirl around and leap so graciously and gracefully away.

And they do this to the tune of music. They have their own musical instruments, and they create many beautiful melodies. In fact, the Strauss waltzes were composed largely as the result of the Ascended Master Saint Germain taking the melodies and rhythms of elemental music and giving them to Johann Strauss by inspiration.

Sometimes the angels orchestrate for them. In fact, the wonderful composer Grieg, in his *Hall of the Mountain King*, captures very well the frenzy of the elementals. If you want to hear elemental life in music, you go and listen to Grieg's, and that particular portion called *The Hall of the Mountain King*, and you will get that feeling.

Elementals are also very, very much in love with violins. They have some of the cutest little violins you ever saw and they play these violins with great rapidity. In fact, it was during the time when Paganini was a boy and was first learning to play, that he made contact with the elementals. This resulted in the very haunting melodies that Paganini played - and of course they tried to say he had a pact with Satan, but this was not true at all. He'd actually contacted the elementals, and some of his haunting music was from the elementals at the time when they were aware of the fact of their own approaching death.

In this haunting music they were trying to create the feeling of immortality. It was a solemn kind of music almost like the Jewish piece, *Kol Nidre*, which is a very beautiful piece. So music has captured a lot of the beauty of the unseen realms for mankind. But we have to enter into the understanding of what it would be like if we did not have all these things.

On the other hand, if we had followed the divine plan, we would be able to see the angels, we would be able to see and be friends with the elementals. We would not have any storms on the planet. The ground would shed forth dew to water our crops. No rain would fall, but dew would appear from the air. The air would be saturated with moisture, in just the right amounts everywhere on earth, and the deserts would bloom as the rose, and there would be no excess moisture, or no lack of it. It would be just right for every climate.

You would have the most beautiful weather, and you would have the most beautiful flowers all over the world, and you would have plenty of food, and you wouldn't find that people would be killing animals to live. There would be an abundant manifestation of fruit. Many of the fruits that would manifest are not even now on the planet. The world would be changed, and we would have communion with the elementals, showing them how to step up into a higher manifestation, and we would be getting our instructions from the angels.

But in order to manifest these conditions, we have to reverse the currents that mankind have created, which have brought about a synthetic concept of the whole picture of what life is and what it should be. And because of this I assure you that those blessed elementals need your help. Because if humanity keep on building layers and layers of erroneous human consciousness to great depth in their world, one of these days you're going to wake up and you're going to find the strata of the rock has upheaved over the continents. The coasts will have cataclysms, you'll find cities destroyed and people in agony, families torn up and disrupted, and you'll find the whole face of the world will be changed. Because the elementals will have a universal upheaval all over the planet. It has happened before, and it can happen again. Because they can only take so much human effluvia in creation and then they have to throw it off.

But what is in the kingdom of God is the positively magnificent, beautiful things that have been the fruit of all great culture from the very beginning of the world. And when we come to the place where the present cycle reaches its end, and we start the golden age cycle, believe you me! we're all going to have to manifest, and the world is going to have to manifest a different face, the different face of creation.

Now this is prophesized, and the Bible prophesizes it where it tells us, "And the day will come when your teachers will no longer be removed into a corner, but you'll be able to see your teachers face to face. And no man will then say to his brother, 'Know God.'" There won't be any preacher standing up and telling you anything, because you will know the truth for yourselves. Everyone will be able to see for themselves the divine Light, and there will be no atheists or agnostics, because they'll all be able to see. They'll all be able to see and talk to the angels and the Ascended Masters. They'll all be able to see and co-operate with the elementals.

And this can happen, and it is divinely intended to happen. But it won't happen automatically or like magic. It will happen if we make it happen, by the right use of our free will in reaching up to the Light, in resurrecting ourselves. The outcome of the equation is up to us, up to you and me. The future of human life, and the future of elemental life, is in our hands this day.

Resources

This is not an exhaustive list of resources on elementals, but covers organisations and activities mentioned in this book.

Books

All books from which I have used extracts are well-worth reading in their entirety, especially those by Dora Van Gelder, Geoffrey Hodson, The Findhorn Community, Tanis Helliwell and Marco Pogacnik. Publisher details can be found in the Bibliography section that follows. The publishers of this book, Capall Bann, also have many other books on fairies and elementals. Refer to their catalogue.

The Findhorn Community is at: The Findhorn Community, The Park, Forres IV36 0TZ, Scotland. Tel: 01309-673655.

For information about the **Zoence** workshops and courses of **Peter Dawkins** write to: Zoence, Roses Farmhouse, Epwell Road, Tysoe, Warwick CV35 0TN, England. Tel: 01295-688185 (+44-1295-688185 from the U.S.A.). E-mail: secretary@zoence.com Web site: http://www.zoence.org.uk

For information about **The Summit Lighthouse** and **The Keepers of the Flame Fraternity** founded by **Mark Prophet**, and which use the science of the spoken Word to work with and to liberate elemental life, write to: The

Summit Lighthouse, P.O. Box 5000, Corwin Springs, MT 59030-5000, U.S.A. Tel: 1-800-245-5445 (406-848-9500 outside the U.S.A.). E-mail: tslinfo@tsl.org Web site: http://www.tsl.org

Bibliography and Reference Notes

By Chapter Number

2. "Hasn't everyone seen fairies?" by Jenny Nisbet, *Daily Mail*, 25 September 1997.

3. Ibid

4. Katherine M. Briggs, *The Fairies in Tradition and Literature*, Routledge and Kegan Paul, London, 1967, p.131.

5. Jenny Nisbet, op. cit.

6. Interview by the author, 1997.

7. *The Life of Benvenuto Cellini Written by Himself*, trans. by John Addington Symonds, Phaidon Press, London, 1949, p.6.

8. Katherine M. Briggs, op. cit., p.162.

9. Walter Gill, *A Second Manx Scrapbook*, Arrowsmith, 1932.

10. Letter in *John O'London's Weekly*, 28 March 1936, p.1023.

11. Katherine M. Briggs, op. cit., pp.19-20.

12. S. John Saunders, "The Invisible Throng," in *The Unknown*,

December 1986, pp.22-25.

13. Katherine M. Briggs, op. cit., pp.131-2.

14. Letter in *Fate* magazine, May 1977, pp.52-3; cited in Janet Bord, *Fairies: Real Encounters with Little People*, Michael O'Mara Books, London, 1997, pp.52-3.

15. *Paracelsus: Of the Supreme Mysteries of Nature*, trans. By R. Turner, pub. By N. Brook and J. Harison, London, 1655, pp.32-3, 51-60; Rosemary Zimmer Bradley, *Encyclopedia of Mystical and Paranormal Experience*, Grange Books, London, 1991; Manley Palmer Hall, *The Secret Teachings of All Ages*, Philosophical Research Society.

16. Dora Van Gelder, *The Real World of Fairies*, Quest Books, Wheaton, Illinois, 1977, pp.10-13, 54-57.

17. Geoffrey Hodson, *Fairies at Work and at Play*, Quest Books, Wheaton, Illinois, 1982 (orig. pub. by Theosophical Publishing House, 1925), pp.58-9, 63-5.

18. Gwen Benwell and Arthur Waugh, *Sea Enchantress*, Hutchinson, London, 1961, p.112.

19. Ibid., p.261.

20. The Findhorn Community, *The Findhorn Garden*, The Findhorn Press, 1975, pp.54, 57.

21. Tanis Helliwell, *Summer With the Leprechauns*, Blue Dolphin Publishing, Nevada City, 1997, pp.4-6.

22. Marko Pogacnik, *Nature Spirits and Elemental Beings*, Findhorn Press, 1996, pp.49-53.

23. Interview by the author, 24 October 1998.

24. This is a 'virtual lecture' by Mark L. Prophet, formed in the following way and for the following reasons. Six unpublished transcripts of Prophet talking about elementals exist, dated: (1) 2 July 1964, (2) July 1964, (3) 12 October 1964, (4) 10 June 1965, (5) 30 November 1969, and (6) 2 July 1972. None of these are in themselves the kind of in-depth or more polished delivery that students of his teachings are used to hearing or reading. The first five are brief introductions to the subject of elementals in order to give a context to the service, prayers or dynamic decrees to follow. All six transcripts have interruptions for public announcements, etc. After consideration, it was clear to me that there were gems of truth among all these transcripts, but no transcript could stand alone in published form. Mark Prophet did have a "matrix" or outline he would tend to follow on this subject. This is best evident in the transcripts numbered above as 1 and 6. By combining the best of these two together, a Prophet lecture worthy of publication began to appear. I have inserted into this key paragraphs from the other four transcripts. A certain amount of editing has naturally been required. This chiefly consists of removing "um's" and "and's", and inserting bridging words or sentences. No factual or informational material whatsoever about elementals has been added by me during the editing process. All of this is from Prophet. Researchers who require the precise, unedited wording of Mark Prophet should refer to the original six transcripts.

Copyright Notices

25 Stop Press Appendix

A Game With the Fairies

Valerie Singleton will need no introduction to any British readers. Having been the most famous presenter of the long-running childrens' TV programme Blue Peter, co-hosting it from 1962-1972, she then went on to present Nationwide, The Money Programme, and BBC Radio 4's PM. Valerie currently has a show on The History Channel. I had come across a mere mention in an old journal that something fairy-like had happened to her, and was able to track her down during her travels. She kindly responded, just in time, for this book.

I cannot remember where exactly I was living, but I do have memories of a very large room with a sofa in the middle of it, and playing a game with my then-nanny and other young friends. The idea was that we would put a series of small objects (a chalk, a button, a thimble) on a nearby sideboard. We would then go and sit on the sofa, all holding hands, so that none of us on the sofa could possibly move any of the small objects, and we would firmly close our eyes. Several minutes later we would open our eyes to find that the objects had been hidden (by the fairies) somewhere in the room and we would then have to find them. As we had all been holding hands, of course it couldn't possibly have been any of us who had hidden the objects and no-one else had come into the room.

My recollection is that one day I cheated and opened my eyes, and I am convinced to this day that I saw several objects flying unaided around the room. I must add that we would play this game in the afternoon, and although we drew the curtains it was a half-light so it was possible to see clearly.

Well, I believe it anyway!

FREE DETAILED CATALOGUE

Capall Bann is owned and run by people actively involved in many of the areas in which we publish. A detailed illustrated catalogue is available on request, SAE or International Postal Coupon appreciated. **Titles can be ordered direct from Capall Bann, post free in the UK** (cheque or PO with order) or from good bookshops and specialist outlets.
Do contact us for details on the latest releases at: **Capall Bann Publishing, Freshfields, Chieveley, Berks, RG20 8TF.** Titles include:

A Breath Behind Time, Terri Hector
Angels and Goddesses - Celtic Christianity & Paganism, M. Howard
Arthur - The Legend Unveiled, C Johnson & E Lung
Astrology The Inner Eye - A Guide in Everyday Language, E Smith
Auguries and Omens - The Magical Lore of Birds, Yvonne Aburrow
Asyniur - Womens Mysteries in the Northern Tradition, S McGrath
Beginnings - Geomancy, Builder's Rites & Electional Astrology in the
    European Tradition, Nigel Pennick
Between Earth and Sky, Julia Day
Caer Sidhe - Celtic Astrology and Astronomy, Vol 1, Michael Bayley
Call of the Horned Piper, Nigel Jackson
Cat's Company, Ann Walker
Celtic Faery Shamanism - The Wisdom of the Otherworld, Catrin James
Celtic Lore & Druidic Ritual, Rhiannon Ryall
Celtic Saints and the Glastonbury Zodiac, Mary Caine
Compleat Vampyre - The Vampyre Shaman, Nigel Jackson
Creating Form From the Mist - The Wisdom of Women in Celtic Myth and
    Culture, Lynne Sinclair-Wood
Crystal Clear - A Guide to Quartz Crystal, Jennifer Dent
Crystal Doorways, Simon & Sue Lilly
Crossing the Borderlines - Guising, Masking & Ritual Animal Disguise in the
    European Tradition, Nigel Pennick
Dragons of the West, Nigel Pennick
Earth Harmony - Places of Power, Holiness & Healing, Nigel Pennick
Eildon Tree (The) Romany Language & Lore, Michael Hoadley
Enchanted Forest - The Magical Lore of Trees, Yvonne Aburrow
Eternally Yours Faithfully, Roy Radford & Evelyn Gregory
Everything You Always Wanted To Know About Your Body, But So Far
    Nobody's Been Able To Tell You, Chris Thomas & D Baker
Face of the Deep - Healing Body & Soul, Penny Allen

Fairies in the Irish Tradition, Molly Gowen
Familiars - Animal Powers of Britain, Anna Franklin
Fool's First Steps, (The) Chris Thomas
Forest Paths - Tree Divination, Brian Harrison, Ill. S. Rouse
From Past to Future Life, Dr Roger Webber
Gardening For Wildlife Ron Wilson
God Year, The, Nigel Pennick & Helen Field
Goddess on the Cross, Dr George Young
Goddess Year, The, Nigel Pennick & Helen Field
Goddesses, Guardians & Groves, Jack Gale
Handbook For Pagan Healers, Liz Joan
Handbook of Fairies, Ronan Coghlan
Healing Book, The, Chris Thomas and Diane Baker
Healing Homes, Jennifer Dent
Healing Journeys, Paul Williamson
Healing Stones, Sue Philips
Herb Craft - Shamanic & Ritual Use of Herbs, Lavender & Franklin
Hub of the Wheel, Skytoucher
In Search of Herne the Hunter, Eric Fitch
Inner Celtia, Alan Richardson & David Annwn
Journey Home, The, Chris Thomas
Language of the Psycards, Berenice
Legend of Robin Hood, The, Richard Rutherford-Moore
Lid Off the Cauldron, Patricia Crowther
Light From the Shadows - Modern Traditional Witchcraft, Gwyn
Living Tarot, Ann Walker
Lore of the Sacred Horse, Marion Davies
Lost Lands & Sunken Cities (2nd ed.), Nigel Pennick
Magical Guardians - Exploring the Spirit and Nature of Trees, Philip Heselton
Magical History of the Horse, Janet Farrar & Virginia Russell
Magical Lore of Animals, Yvonne Aburrow
Magical Lore of Cats, Marion Davies
Magical Lore of Herbs, Marion Davies
Medium Rare - Reminiscences of a Clairvoyant, Muriel Renard
Mind Massage - 60 Creative Visualisations, Marlene Maundrill
Moon Mysteries, Jan Brodie
Mysteries of the Runes, Michael Howard
Mystic Life of Animals, Ann Walker
New Celtic Oracle The, Nigel Pennick & Nigel Jackson
Pagan Feasts - Seasonal Food for the 8 Festivals, Franklin & Phillips
Patchwork of Magic - Living in a Pagan World, Julia Day
Places of Pilgrimage and Healing, Adrian Cooper
Practical Meditation, Steve Hounsome
Practical Spirituality, Steve Hounsome
Psychic Self Defence - Real Solutions, Jan Brodie
Real Fairies, David Tame

FREE detailed catalogue and FREE 'Inspiration' magazine

Contact: Capall Bann Publishing, Freshfields, Chieveley, Berks, RG20 8TF